COVER:

North, or entrance, front of Mount Clare. The main block of the house was constructed between 1757 and 1760. The brick walls are laid in an irregular Flemish bond. The tops of the chimneys and the gable ends of the roof were altered in 1890. The window sashes are twentieth century replacements in nineteenth century frames. The portico, or piazza, with a sitting room above was built in 1768 in carefully laid Flemish bond. The stone columns and paving for the portico were ordered from England in 1767. The Palladian window is one of the earliest constructed on a residence in Maryland. The entrance door is surrounded by rustication, and the wall sheltered by the portico is stuccoed. The hyphens and wings were built in 1908 to replace the original ones which were demolished circa 1873. *Photograph by Marion E. Warren.*

FRONT END LEAF:

South elevation of Mount Clare, as it appeared in 1770. From the orangery on the left to the wash house balancing it on the right, the house with its connected dependencies extended 240 feet. The small dependency between the wash and the kitchen wing is believed to have been the ice house. The use of the balancing dependency between the orangery and the office wing is unknown. *Drawing by author.*

I

⌐⌐⌐ Charles Carroll, Barrister (1723-1783) by John Hesselius (1728-1778) circa 1760. Oil on canvas, 30 inches by 25 inches. This painting shows the Barrister as he appeared at the time he was building Mount Clare. The frame is believed to be the one he ordered from London in September 1761. *Collection of Mrs. Bartow Van Ness, Jr. Photograph by Duane Suter.*

II

MOUNT CLARE

Being an Account of the Seat built by Charles Carroll, Barrister, upon his Lands at Patapsco

BY

MICHAEL F. TROSTEL, A.I.A.

FOR

THE NATIONAL SOCIETY OF THE COLONIAL DAMES OF AMERICA
IN THE STATE OF MARYLAND

Bookplate of Charles Carroll, Barrister.

Library Of Congress Catalog Card No.:
81-82385

Trostel, Michael F.

Mount Clare, Being an Account of the Seat
built by Charles Carroll, Barrister,
upon his Lands at Patapsco.

Baltimore: National Society of Colonial Dames of America
in the State of Maryland
144 p.
8107   810527

CONTENTS

LIST OF
ILLUSTRATIONS

ACKNOWLEDGMENTS

As first envisioned in the spring of 1974, this work was to deal exclusively with the architectural development of Mount Clare, but it soon became apparent that its scope had to be expanded. Brian de Breffny and Rosemary ffolliott succinctly stated the case in the Foreword of their book, *The Houses of Ireland*, published by Thames & Hudson in 1975, saying:

> The history of a house should not be separated from that of the people who built and lived in it, and thus domestic architecture cannot be divorced from family history, social history or political events. Dates of marriage, of inheritance or of local troubles, for example, have a vital bearing on dates of building and rebuilding.

Such a history cannot be accomplished by one person working alone, and I cannot sufficiently express my appreciation to all those who proffered information and encouragement and suggested avenues of study based upon their own research and knowledge.

The following institutions were generous in making their libraries and collections available: the Evergreen Foundation, the Equitable Society of Baltimore, the George Peabody Department of the Enoch Pratt Free Library, Historic Annapolis, Inc., The Milton S. Eisenhower Library of The Johns Hopkins University, the Maryland Historical Trust, the Maryland State Library, the Pennsylvania Historical Society, and the Henry Francis du Pont Winterthur Museum. Most especially, I would like to thank the staffs at the Hall of Records of the State of Maryland, the Library and Manuscript Department of the Maryland Historical Society, and the Maryland Room of the Enoch Pratt Free Library in Baltimore for their unfailing courtesy and assistance.

The owners of a number of houses important to this study graciously opened their doors to me: Mr. and Mrs. Coleman du Pont at the Dr. Upton Scott house; Mr. and Mrs. John Thorpe Richards of the John Ridout house, which was built by Mr. Richards's great-great-great-great grandfather; and the late Mr. and Mrs. W. Flaccus Stifel at Hope House in Talbot County. Mr.

Yvon Kirkpatrick-Howath kindly permitted me to explore the ruins of Squirrel Neck overlooking the Rhode River.

I am indebted to Brice M. Clagett and Mrs. William C. Trimble for making available their papers on the Carroll family, and to Dr. and Mrs. R. Carmichael Tilghman and Mrs. Thomas B. Cockey for helping me through the labyrinth of the Lloyd and Tilghman relationships.

Among the many individuals who provided guidance and important facts, I must acknowledge: Orin M. Bullock, Jr., F.A.I.A., James D. Dilts, John R. Dorsey, William Voss Elder III, Robert L. Eney, Walter S. Furlow, Jr., Henry Chandlee Foreman, F.A.I.A., Eugenia Calvert Holland, Richard H. Howland, Bryden B. Hyde, F.A.I.A., the late Henry W. Keating and the late Mrs. Keating, Edward C. Papenfuse, F. Garner Ranney, Philip M. Reitzel, Orlando Ridout IV, Levin Gale Shreve, Frank S. Welsh, Charles R. Wineberg, Jr. and Mrs. Thomas G. Young III.

I am grateful to Mary Louise Huovinen for translating my handwriting into legible, typed drafts. My thanks also to Phebe R. Jacobsen, Thomas H. Powell, and Mr. and Mrs. Theron K. Rinehart, who read the manuscript and made many invaluable suggestions, and to James F. Waesche, whose editorial assistance was essential.

Finally, I must express my appreciation to the Architectural and Archaeological Survey Committee of the National Society of the Colonial Dames of America in the State of Maryland, under the chairmanship of Mrs. William R. Miller, who never waivered in their faith that this history would one day be completed.

MICHAEL F. TROSTEL

Baltimore, Maryland

May 1981

ACKNOWLEDGEMENTS

Detail of the aquatint *East View of Baltimore Maryland* drawn by G. Beck, Philadelphia. Engraved by T. Cartwrite, London. Published January 1st 1802 by Atkins & Nightingale, 17½ inches by 22½ inches. This is the earliest known printed view of Baltimore and is based on a landscape by George Beck, painted in 1796-1797. The team of horses and wagon are approaching Baltimore along the Frederick Road and at the bottom of the hill will ford the Gwynns Falls. The mill building on the near side of the stream is on the Baltimore Company's property. The land across Gwynns Falls and to the right of the Frederick Road is part of Mount Clare. The mansion is out of sight, set in the trees behind the mill. *Collection of the Peale Museum.*

PROLOGUE

The history of the Carrolls at Mount Clare began on the eleventh of July 1732 when Dr. Charles Carroll took up a patent on 2,368 acres which he called Georgia. The land lay along the Middle Branch of the Patapsco River in Baltimore County. Gwynns Falls ran down through the tract, and where the falls met the river, there was deep water suitable for anchoring ocean-going vessels. The Georgia patent was mostly forested and, as early as 1719, Peter Bond had established a saw mill along Gwynns Falls. Dr. Carroll's interest in the property, however, was in the valuable deposits of iron ore that the land was known to contain.

While Dr. Carroll had been trained as a physician, he was a man of many interests, among which was land speculation. In an age before there were banks or a stock exchange, Dr. Carroll, like many others, invested his cash in real estate. By 1732 he already owned several tracts adjoining his Georgia patent as well as holding land in other parts of Maryland.

In October 1731, soon after the iron ore found along Gwynns Falls was determined to be of an economically profitable grade, the Baltimore Company had been founded. The enterprise, also referred to as the Baltimore Iron Works, was established by Dr. Carroll, Charles Carroll of Annapolis and his brother Daniel Carroll of Duddington, Daniel Dulany and Benjamin Tasker. Each man held a one-fifth interest in the company and Dr. Carroll was to be responsible for its management. The next year, in assembling land for the iron works, Dr. Carroll sold 2,513 acres to the Baltimore Company. Included among the parcels of land he sold was "Georgia, that part thereof on the West Side of the Falls" comprising 1,568 acres of the tract he had recently patented.

On his remaining 800 acres, Dr. Carroll established a plantation and other enterprises. He had a grist mill in operation along the east side of Gwynns Falls by 1733 and on the point of land where the falls emptied into the river, the doctor built a shipyard.

At that time, and until the middle of the nineteenth century, the edge of the river reached up to the line of present day Ridgely Street. Carroll's Point, where the shipyard was located, was at the site of Russell Street between Bayard and Worcester. Forming the north side of the Point was

Three Prong Branch. Carroll's Branch, which flowed into it, ran northward and ended near Baltimore and Poppleton Streets. Another creek ran northwest between Bayard and Bush Streets.

Dr. Carroll's remaining portion of the Georgia patent was an irregularly shaped tract which can be traced only with difficulty on the street map of present day Baltimore. Its boundary ran west from Carroll's Point along the Middle Branch of the Patapsco River, followed up the east side of Gwynns Falls to the Frederick Road, and turned northeast along that road. The northern edge of the plantation was near Lombard and Payson Streets. The property line ran east near the present Pratt Street and at Poppleton dropped down across the Washington Boulevard to Carroll Street. Here, the line turned west to the creek between Bayard and Bush Streets and then ran southeast along the creek to Severn Street where it met the Three Prong Branch and Carroll's Point.

There was an existing road across the property, part of the seventeenth century highway that wound down from Pennsylvania. The road crossed Jones Falls near the head of the North Branch of the Patapsco where Baltimore Town was being established; it then divided in two, one route heading west and the other south, crossing the Patapsco River at Elk Ridge and on to Annapolis, the capital of the province. The Elk Ridge road ran fairly close to the edge of the river on the doctor's land and was often impassable due to the marshy soil near the water. In 1738 Dr. Carroll tried to improve the road, but without success, and in 1750 rerouted it on higher ground through the northern part of his property. The new road followed the line of today's Cole Street and near the intersection of Cole and Monroe Streets angled southwest, crossing Gwynns Falls at what is now called the Old Georgetown Road. It was this route that Washington traveled so many times, and along this road that Rochambeau's army marched on its way to Yorktown.

In the late 1740's Dr. Carroll decided to increase his business operations on the Georgia tract. At the same time, he built a small, one-and-a-half story house for his family's use. The site was on the edge of a hill overlooking his fields and meadows, with a view stretching down the river toward the Chesapeake Bay.

Two miles from the gates leading to this new house, through wooded countryside, lay Baltimore Town, a bustling, overgrown village with a population of barely five hundred people.

This was the beginning of the plantation known as Mount Clare and the setting for the country house the doctor's son, Charles Carroll, Barrister, began to build in 1756.

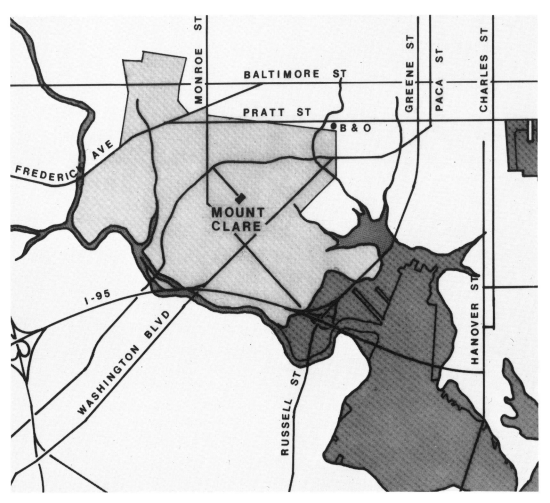

Map of southwest Baltimore showing the extent of the Mount Clare estate circa 1800 and the original shore line. The 800 acres of the Georgia patent retained by Dr. Charles Carroll plus 205 acres added by his son and grandson are indicated by the shaded area. The eighteenth century highway is shown crossing the property and the lane leading from it to the house. *Drawing by author.*

Dr. Charles Carroll's house at Main and Conduit Streets in Annapolis, built circa 1724. Detail of a pencil sketch by Francis B. Mayer (1827-1899), circa 1874. From Dr. Tuck's house on State Circle, Mayer sketched the view down Main Street with the Carroll house in the foreground. Behind it are the roof and chimneys of the City Hotel and in the distance is seen the mouth of the Severn River. *From the Francis B. Mayer sketch books in the collection of the Maryland State Library. Photograph by Marion E. Warren.*

I

THE FAMILY

In 1766 Charles Carroll, writing from his residence in Annapolis to the wine merchants Scott Pringle and Company in Madeira, said:

> There are so many of the name in this Town that some Particular Distinction is necessary to Prevent mistakes please therefore to Direct to me Councellor or Barrister at Law.

A "Particular Distinction" was indeed necessary. At the time the Barrister was writing, there were three other Charles Carrolls living in Annapolis and on nearby plantations, and each was prominent in the economic and social life of the province.

The first Carroll in Maryland was Charles Carroll who arrived in 1688, and was known as "The Settler." He was the second son of Daniel Carroll of Litterluna, King's County, Ireland, and the father of Charles Carroll of Annapolis and Daniel Carroll of Duddington. One of his grandsons was Charles Carroll of Carrollton, a signer of the Declaration of Independence. Other Carrolls, also descended from Daniel Carroll of Litterluna, settled in All Hollows Parish, Anne Arundel County.

Another family of Carrolls in Maryland was descended from Daniel Carroll of Upper Marlboro in Prince George's County. One of his sons married a granddaughter of Charles Carroll the Settler, and another was Archbishop John Carroll, the first Roman Catholic prelate in the United States.

There was also Captain Henry Carroll of Calvert County, who later moved to the Eastern Shore. From him were descended Governor Thomas King Carroll and Anna Ella Carroll, an influential political writer and pamphleteer in the 1850's and 60's.

Sometime between 1712 and 1715, Dr. Charles Carroll arrived in Annapolis. He was the son of Charles Carroll and Clare Dunn of Clonlisk, King's County, Ireland, and a distant cousin of Charles Carroll the Settler. Dr. Charles Carroll's family had lost their land in Ireland during the politically stormy era between the Civil War in the 1640's and the Battle of the Boyne in 1690. In 1748, Dr. Carroll—replying to a letter from a distant cousin, Sir Daniel O'Carroll, in London—wrote:

> My Brother John some Years ago had resolved to go to the West Indies, Spanish Islands, and main; and in his Passige with other Gentlemen from Barbadoes to Anteago the Vessell and all were Lost, wch Leaves me the onely son of the Famely you mention but by this I do not Expect to Inherit Clanlisk, Ballibrit, Leap, Castle Town, or any other Part or a Foot in Ely O'Carroll. Transplantations sequestrations, Acts of Settlement, Explanations, Infamous Informations for Loyalty & other Evils forbid.[1]

The doctor's grandfather was John O'Carroll of Clonlisk, who married Mary Dillon, a granddaughter of the first Viscount Dillon. In 1691 John O'Carroll lost the bulk of his estate as a result of his support of King James II at the Battle of the Boyne. His father, also named John, had been a ward of King James I during his minority and was the last of the O'Carrolls to be recognized as the Chief of Ely O'Carroll, the senior branch of the O'Carroll family. (Cromwell forced the Irish chiefs to drop their titles after he invaded Ireland in 1649 and they were not resumed after the Restoration.) The elder John O'Carroll had married Eleanor Butler, who was descended from the Earls of Ormond and Ossory.

Several years after his arrival in Maryland, Dr. Carroll married Dorothy Blake, daughter of Charles Blake of Queen Anne's County and his wife, Henrietta Lloyd. Dorothy Blake was also a niece of Richard Bennett, who was considered to be the wealthiest man in Maryland at the beginning of the eighteenth century. Thus through his marriage, the doctor became allied with some of the most influential families in the province. The Blakes and the Bennetts were also two of the most prominent Roman Catholic families in Maryland.

On Sunday, the twenty-second of March 1723, a son — named Charles for his father and grandfather — was born to Dr. and Mrs. Carroll. In 1727 they had a daughter, Mary Clare, and four years later a second son, John Henry, was born.

The same year as his elder son's birth, Dr. Carroll purchased the lot at the southwest corner of Conduit and Church (now Main) Streets in Annapolis from Thomas Bladen for £50 and built a residence to house his growing family. The two-and-a-half story clapboarded house is still standing. It is T-shaped, with three tall chimneys continuing above the brick end walls. The parlor is one of the earliest surviving paneled rooms in Annapolis.[2] The house was evidently completed in 1727, because in July of that year, Dr. Carroll ordered, through Capt. John Hyde in London,

> 1 Doz Strong Russia Leather Chairs of about 9^s a piece a Strong Couch & two Arm Chairs to match half a Doz^n Cane Chairs of about 7^s a piece

This house remained in the family until 1820 when it was sold by James Carroll, one of the doctor's grandsons.[3]

Dr. Carroll was ambitious for his family and, as his land, shipping, and mercantile investments prospered, he determined to give his elder son as good an education as possible. Accordingly, he embarked with the ten-year-old boy for Europe, where Charles was to be placed in school. During the voyage, their ship encountered such heavy storms that it was blown off course and the passengers landed in Portugal instead of England. Dr. Carroll later wrote:

> In the year 1734 I was with my Son put in (by the Stress at Sea) to Lisbon and the Child being much Fatigued with the Voyage I left him there at the English College in Bailo Alt under the Care of Mr. Edward Jones the President of the Same College.

Young Charles Carroll remained at the English College for four years. On June 30, 1738 his father wrote to his London agent, Samuel Hyde, to arrange for the boy's passage to England and to place him in Eton.[4] Dr. Carroll instructed Mr. Hyde that his son was to receive an allowance of two shillings a week. While commenting on the need to be frugal, he directed that:

> the expense be no greater than is absolutely necessary on the occasion . . . and let him know (as in fact the case is) that he is to depend on nothing more frome me, than a foundation of learning for some profession to get his bread hereafter.

Following Eton, Charles Carroll entered Clare College, Cambridge. His father increased his allowance to five pounds per quarter, saying:

View of King's College and Clare College from the Back Lawn of King's, Cambridge. Watercolor by Thomas Rowlandson (1756-1827). To the left of the chapel is seen part of Clare College which Charles Carroll attended from 1742 to 1746. *Courtesy of the Syndics of the Fitzwilliam Museum.*

> This Money I hope you will layout in Nessaries for your Person, or Endowment of Your Mind & not spend in Wine or Riot. Remark, that Women & Wine are the Bane of Youth—

Yet in the same letter he urged his son to "Pray take opportunities to Improve your Dancing." The doctor ended with comments that every father has made to his son in college since time immemorial: "I am sorry to hear that you are not more careful of your Cloths and that you incline too much to Company."

In the summer of 1746, having been away from his family for twelve years, Charles Carroll returned to Annapolis. The most important changes Charles encountered on his arrival were those which had occurred within his own family. His mother, Dorothy Blake Carroll, had died in 1734, six months after he had left for school in Europe.[5] Three years later, his father had remarried. Dr. Carroll's second wife was Anne Plater, the daughter of George Plater, who had been Attorney-General of Maryland from 1691 to 1698. Her brother, George Plater II, built Sotterley, in Saint Mary's County.[6] Through the Platers, the Carrolls were now part of another network of family and financial connections. Anne Plater Carroll's four nieces (and thus young Charles Carroll's stepcousins) married members of prominent Virginia families. One was the wife of William Gooch, whose father, Sir William Gooch, was governor of Virginia from 1727 to 1749. Another niece married Col. John Tayloe of Richmond County, who had interests in iron furnaces as well as large land holdings in that colony and Maryland. He was the builder of Mount Airy, the greatest of the Palladian mansions in Virginia. Among the Carroll papers are copies of both business and social correspondence with John Tayloe. Later, the families would be further connected with the marriage of one of the Tayloes' daughters to Charles Carroll's cousin, Edward Lloyd IV.

The mid-1740's were a difficult time for Dr. Carroll, as they were for all American merchants and planters. England was at war with France and Spain. Ships had to cross the Atlantic in convoys. The coasts of America were still being attacked by pirates. In the midst of this danger and uncertainty, Dr. Carroll could not depend upon getting his iron and tobacco to England. Several times, his vessels sailing to the Barbados were chased by privateers. Some of his ships were lost, and insurance rates were high.

Charles Carroll was put to work by his father assisting him in his many, involved business ventures. The doctor was not displeased with the results of his son's English education and obviously had hopes for the young man's future, which he expressed in a letter written in August, 1746 to William Black in London:

> I . . . am obliged for your kind Sentiments of him; He is a sober Discreet Youth & has a good foundation of Learning and Judgement for any Profession, but these times are so difficult y^d I fear shall not be able to Procure money to send him Back again; If times Change and can get our Effects to Market and they answer, may be able to do something for him otherwise he must take his Chance here.[7]

Yet at this same period when Dr. Carroll was worrying over hard times and his letters were filled with business problems and comments upon the need to "Act with Utmost Frugality" he sent orders for wines from Madeira and "Pine appels" from Barbados. From England, he ordered twenty pounds of hair powder and two powder puffs. High heeled silk shoes, "A Nosegay artificial Flowers Six Shillings Value," and "Genteel Fans" were needed from London for his wife and daughter. A little later, for Mrs. Carroll, he ordered a flowered silk nightgown of salmon colored background, Spanish leather shoes with high heels and a "Genteel Fashionable Mob with an Edging of about 5/ a yard Made to Suit a woman of fifty years old."

In 1747 Mary Clare Carroll married Nicholas Maccubbin, a young Annapolis merchant. The doctor's son-in-law came from a family which had been established in Anne Arundel County for several generations. From each of his parents Nicholas Maccubbin had inherited plantations on the Rhode River below Annapolis. As part of her dowry, Mary Clare Carroll brought her husband 1,500 acres in Prince George's County and a wharf with a warehouse on the harbor at Annapolis.

Whether by coincidence or design, Dr. Carroll sold his house on the corner of Church and Conduit Streets on June 21, 1746 for £600 to Benjamin Young, who in turn sold it on June 24 to

Portrait thought to be of Mary Clare Carroll Maccubbin (1727-1781) by John Hesselius (1728-1778), circa 1758. Oil on canvas, 30 inches by 25 inches. Until recently, the sitter was believed to be Dorothy Blake Carroll (1702-1734), but recent research into eighteenth century clothing styles has ruled out this possibility. The portrait has always been known to be of a member of Dr. Charles Carroll's family and because the subject's facial characteristics are close to those of Charles Carroll, Barrister, it is now thought that the portrait is of his sister, Mary Clare. *Collection of Mrs. Aubrey Pearre. Photography by Duane Suter.*

Nicholas Maccubbin for £550. Thus Mary Clare Carroll Maccubbin returned as a bride to the house in which she had been raised. In time her children and grandchildren would also live there.

Dr. Carroll had purchased a number of Annapolis lots from the heirs of Amos Garrett in the 1730's. The lots totaled something over seven acres and lay between Duke of Gloucester Street and the Market Place on the waterfront. Dr. Carroll laid out Green Street through the property and advertised to sell lots along the new street in 1749. There was an existing house on the east side of the new street into which the doctor had moved his family. This was a clapboarded house, a story-and-a-half high with a gambrel roof, which sat back from Green Street in the midst of several acres. A pair of parlors stretched across the back. From the windows, the Carrolls could look out across Horn Point to the mouth of the Severn River and the Chesapeake Bay beyond. On the edge of his property, by the harbor, Dr. Carroll had a dock and a warehouse next to the one that was part of his daughter's dowry. Until John Ridout built his house on Duke of Gloucester Street in the middle of the 1760's, Dr. Carroll's house sat alone on the hill overlooking the Annapolis harbor and must have been a landmark with its five chimneys rising above the treetops.

When the Peace of Aix-la-Chappelle ended the War of the Austrian Succession in 1748, the economy of Britain's colonies prospered again. Dr. Carroll was full of plans. He invested heavily in land in what was later to become Frederick County. He began building more ships at his yard on Carroll's Point on the Patapsco River, and he considered erecting an iron furnace on the east side of Gwynns Falls, opposite the Baltimore Company's works.

On April 17, 1749 Dr. Carroll gave his elder son his plantation in upper Baltimore County called The Caves. The doctor had begun assembling this land in 1730 with the purchase of 972 acres called Coales Caves. At the time he made the property over to Charles, The Caves totaled 1,770 acres. With the help of two overseers, Charles managed this plantation while continuing to assist his father in the family's shipping, commercial, land and iron ventures.

In November of the same year, Dr. Carroll sent his younger son, eighteen-year-old John Henry, to Philadelphia, "to acquire Knowledge in mercantile affairs." "Jackey" Carroll was placed under the merchant Reese Meredith with whom both Dr. Carroll and Nicholas Maccubbin had business affiliations.

In Philadelphia, John Henry lodged "at Widdow Gibs next Door but one to the Academy in fourth Street." The doctor admonished his son to "pray take Good Care of your Things and keep an Exact Account of y^r Linnen going to Wash & Receiving the same." And while he was away from home, Jackey was reminded to "take a Care to get a Seat in the Church to pay Your Duty to God which I hope you will always mind, as the Principal of all Duties." However, Dr. Carroll realized that the young man's life would not be all work and attention to duty, so in a trunk, along with a number of books Jackey needed, he enclosed a velvet riding cap his son had left behind in Annapolis.

By the late 1740's Dr. Carroll was increasingly occupied with his business activities in the Upper Chesapeake Bay region—his interest in the Baltimore Company, ship building at Carroll's Point, a grist mill on Gwynns Falls, farming operations on the Georgia tract and also on Carroll's Island, a 1,000 acre plantation at the mouth of the Gunpowder River. While planning his proposed iron furnace on Gwynns Falls, Dr. Carroll decided to build a house for his use when in the area. The site he chose was on his Georgia patent, on the edge of the first rise of land behind the Middle Branch of the Patapsco River with a superb view down the river to the Chesapeake Bay.

Among the Carroll-Maccubbin papers at the Maryland Historical Society is a memorandum in the doctor's handwriting starting with the "Cost of a furnace 24 by 26 feet Square." After notes about the cost of the iron furnace, Dr. Carroll wrote:

To Charges in building a good framed house 50 feet long 20 feet wide, stack of chimnies with 4 fire places	£150
Ware house, Stables & Kitchen	100
Cole houses & Corn Room	50
	300

The later houses may be built while the stone is digging and bringing to place or
other materials for ye furnace.

This story-and-a-half, clapboarded house was the original house built for the Carroll family on
their land "at Patapsco."

In November 1749 Dr. Carroll started ordering materials for his iron furnace and house on
the Georgia tract "on Patapsco." The following spring he ordered 3,000 feet of one-inch pine
planks. In July 1751, he commented upon his need for cash to pay for the iron furnace and other
construction at Georgia and for land purchases. Later that year the doctor ordered furnishings and
cutlery which were probably for the new house.

When young Charles Carroll had completed his studies at Cambridge in 1746, William
Black, one of his father's London agents, had urged Dr. Carroll to let his son remain in England,
but Charles had sailed for Annapolis. Now, as part of his plans for his family's future, the doctor
made arrangements for his elder son to return to England. On August 18, 1751 he wrote to Mr.
Black:

S^r
    You heretofore wrote that I had better let my son take his Chance in Britain, And as Planting
will not do without some other Business or Professions, and the Law being the most thriveing
here he has determined to Read it for some time in the Temple so as to Qualefie himself for the
Practice and as he has a good Foundation of Learning and Natural and Acquired knowledge; I
have no Reson to doubt but he will make a good proficiency therein.
    I have that opinion of his Prudence and good management that I hope he will Act with utmost
Frugality.
    He will want some money to Purchase Books and Furniture for a Room as allso for other
Requisites wch I desire you will advance for him not Exceeding Three hundred Pounds In any
one year, for wch I shall take care to make Remittance so as you may not be long in Advance.
    In case you are Out of Your money I will with pleasure allow you five p^rCent Interest
Annualy for the same and I Doubt not but you will Deem him and me good Security, he him
self having a Seat of Very Good Land here and Two good plantations with a Dozen Working
hands the produce of wch will be Yearly Remitted to you.
    I have so great dependence on Your Friendship on this Ocation that I put my Son under your
Protection. And am with True Respect

Sir
Your Most Humble
Servant
Charles Carroll

Young Charles sailed from Annapolis the same month despite the family's worries about
Spanish pirates. When he reached London he settled into chambers at Library Stair Case No. 2,
Garden Court at the Middle Temple and began reading law.

With all of his children away, Dr. Carroll suddenly felt the passage of time, commenting that
"My Family is now Reduced to very few . . . none but my Wife and my Self."

The following winter, the doctor was greatly concerned when he learned that Charles was ill
in London. All his life, Charles would be plagued by ill health. It has always been thought that the
"auges and feavers" he complained of were a form of malaria which he contracted while a student
in Portugal. In a long letter Doctor Carroll sent medical advice and urged his son to "Be not
Melancholly" or dispirited. If necessary "Charlie" should take time away from his studies to try
the waters at Bath. After all, as the doctor pointed out, "Books may be there Read."

In the early 1750's the doctor was embroiled in a bitter quarrel with Charles Carroll of Annapolis over the estate of James Carroll of Anne Arundel County of which Dr. Carroll was the executor. Charles Carroll of Annapolis was a second cousin of the late James Carroll and distantly related to Dr. Carroll. He was also one of the doctor's partners in the Baltimore Company and a neighbor in Annapolis. During the controversy, Dr. Carroll consulted Daniel Dulany, another of the five owners of the iron works, for legal advice. James Carroll had died in 1728 and the quarrel between the men had been growing since that time. The ill will between the two Charles Carrolls was heightened because Dr. Carroll and his children had become members of the Church of England while Charles Carroll of Annapolis and his family remained staunch Roman Catholics. Thus when, in 1752, the other partners in the Baltimore Company forced Dr. Carroll to stop his competing iron furnace operations on the opposite side of Gwynns Falls from the Company's works, the doctor believed this was caused by the animosity of Charles Carroll of Annapolis.

Nothing daunted, Dr. Carroll made other plans for the iron furnace site and on February 2, 1753 wrote to his elder son at the Middle Temple in London:

> . . . your Brother is returned from Philadelphia, . . . I think to Settle him at Patapsco to build a Merchant Mill there; and make it a Center for my Business, to have Taylor Shoemakers and other Supplys for my Quarters there under his Care and Management and allow him one Moiey of any Profits arising which I hope may turn to advantage to us both as I propose baking Ship Bread there with other Business . . .
>
> You are Sensible that the Two Fires which destroyed my Warehouse & Bakehouse with my Losses in the last war, obliged me to sell the Interest I had at North East in Baltimore County For a Furnace with Sufficient Quantity of ore Wood & other Supplys to last for ever to Neal & C° which is now the property of Dr Nich^s Hacket Carew & C°. . . .[8]
>
> . . . Implacable Malice of some here ag^t me which laid me under a Necessity of pulling down my Furnace at Patapsco, before it made Pig Iron to pay the Charge of erecting it and this by the popish Int: combined ag^t me, however as I would make the best of it. It is that Furnace Wheels & site thereof I am converting into a Merch^t Mill which I expect to go this next Fall. . . .
>
> I have great Hopes of Y^r Brothers Conduct and Assistance, and You are Sensible of the Dependance on you therefore shall not enlarge on that Subject.
>
> If I am not so happy as to bring this Matter to perfection in my Life Time which still I hope to do Yet I will leave the Plan to you and Your Brother and am certain with the Foundation I have laid it will be Accomplished with Ease. . . .
>
> I built Two Tobacco Houses & a Barn at Your Quarters this last Year Your overseers have made a pretty good Crops. I have ordered them to get their Tobacco ready as soon as they Can. Judd left Two Hogshs of Tobacco at the Inspecting House In Baltimore Town last Year but shall be shiped this.
>
> I cannot see that by making Tobacco I should better my own Yours or Your Bro^s Fortunes & that induces me to go upon the Iron Business and making Grain to Support it.

The doctor's hopes and plans for his two sons to carry on his ventures crumbled the next year with the death of his younger son on the fifteenth of February 1754. On February 21 the *Maryland Gazette* announced "Last Friday died, at his Father's House in this City, aged 22 Years, of a confirm'd Consumption, Mr. JOHN HENRY CARROLL, youngest son of Dr. CHARLES CARROLL."

The doctor himself was not in good health, and his son's death was a severe blow. He wrote to his surviving son in London, begging him to return, saying, "I am now wishing to have you here with me least my Eyes should Close before I see you they began to be dim long since but this last stroke has added Dimness to my Sight & Senses." A few months later, Dr. Carroll wrote again to tell Charles that he should remain at the Temple for a full three years, that period being "full sufficient to Qualifie for Plantations practice." Following his father's wishes, he continued in England until the following summer when he took passage on the ship *Buchanan*. In June 1755, after a voyage of nine weeks, Charles Carroll arrived home in Annapolis.

Dr. Carroll never recovered from John Henry's death. The grief he expressed in his private papers shows how deeply he loved his children. He had lived with the wish of seeing his surviving son return and with that desire fulfilled, the doctor died at his house on Green Street, three months later; on September twenty-ninth, at the age of 64.[9]

At the time of his death, the *Maryland Gazette* described Dr. Carroll as "a gentleman of good sense and breeding, courteous and affable." In addition to his medical practice and his business ventures, the doctor had served as a vestryman and a warden of St. Anne's Church in Annapolis, and from 1737 until his death he had represented Anne Arundel County in the lower house of the provincial assembly.

In his will, Dr. Carroll left his wife 50 pounds sterling a year in accordance with the settlement made at the time of their marriage, and each member of his daughter's family was left 10 pounds with which to buy mourning. All the rest of the doctor's considerable estate passed to his surviving son.

This son, who was now styled "Charles Carroll, Esq. of the Law" or more simply "Charles Carroll, Barrister," found himself at the age of 32 to be one of the half-dozen wealthiest men in Maryland.

II

THE HOUSE
1756-1766

Within a few months of coming into his inheritance, Charles Carroll, Barrister, must have determined to build a new and larger house at his plantation on the Patapsco River. During the summer of 1756, less than a year after his father's death, he began ordering materials from England. The first invoice included glass for the windows — 457 pieces nine by eleven inches, and 244 pieces seven by nine inches — indicating that the design of the house and its dependencies had been settled.

The plan called for demolishing the one-and-a-half story house built by Dr. Carroll a few years earlier and constructing a new one on the same site. The location, overlooking the river with the Chesapeake Bay in the distance, could not be equaled at any other site on the estate. Also, the view of the new house, planned with a row of outbuildings stretching to each side in a balanced composition along the top of the hill, would be an impressive sight to ships coming up the Patapsco.

Later in the summer of 1756, the Barrister wrote again to John Steuart & Company to add iron H hinges and boxlocks for the bedchambers and brass H hinges and boxlocks for the first floor rooms to his first order. These, in addition to the hardware in the existing house, would be enough for the new one.

It was at least six months and often a year before goods ordered from England could be expected to arrive in the colonies. In late October 1757, the Barrister wrote inquiring about the building materials he had sent for more than 14 months earlier, saying that he was in great need of them. When the glass finally arrived the next year, Charles Carroll wrote in annoyance to Steuart that "the Glass. . . Bought of Elizabeth Adams was but Bristol Glass tho' she Charges me with best Crown Glass and I think she should Refund the Difference."

Staircase seen through arch. The moulded arch supported by triple clustered pilasters is the most elaborate woodwork remaining from the original construction period of the house. The tall case clock is similar to the one that stood in the same location on the stair during Charles Carroll's lifetime. *Photograph by Marion E. Warren.*

The same day, August 20, 1758, Carroll wrote to another London merchant for 300[lb] Weight of sheet Lead fit for Lining the Gutters of a House." The new correspondent was William Anderson, a former ship's captain who had married Rebecca Lloyd from Talbot County. Through his wife's connections, Anderson acted as the London agent for many prominent Maryland families. In late 1756 Carroll had begun shipping iron to William Anderson, using him for banking and other financial services, and ordering goods through him. By 1759 all of the Barrister's invoices for furniture, silver, clothing and other stylish or fine quality goods went to Anderson in London.

The only materials for the new house ordered directly from England by the Barrister were window glass, sheet lead, hinges, locks, and nails. These were items needed in quantity and not manufactured in America, and it was cheaper to order them directly from abroad. When the nails and hardware did not at first arrive, he wrote: "As from your Delay to send me in proper time the Goods wrote for to you . . . I have been obliged to supply myself with them at an Extravagant advance here in the Country." Other building materials were available through Annapolis merchants. Carroll, most probably, would have purchased them from his brother-in-law, Nicholas Maccubbin, one of the largest merchants in the capital.

The wood for joists and floor boards 'and shingles must have come from commercial sawmills. It was usual to let lumber dry for several years before using it for construction, and since the Barrister made his plans and began to build quickly, there was not enough time for lumber sawn from trees on his own properties to be thoroughly seasoned. When Dr. Carroll built the first house on the site, he had purchased boards from a merchant across the Bay in Dorchester County.

Most of the bricks for the house would have been made on the plantation. In Tidewater Maryland and Virginia, it was customary to hire a gang of brickmakers to build a kiln near a building site and, using the clay dug nearby, make the necessary number of bricks. On the Barrister's property there were abundant clay deposits in the low land between the Patapsco River and the hill on which the new house was rising. The mortar, too, would have been locally produced from oyster shells and marl, which, when burned and slaked with water, made excellent mortar. Besides those made on the plantation, there were commercially made bricks available nearby. The accounts of a Baltimore merchant, Mark Alexander, show that he sold 500 bricks to Charles Carroll on January 10, 1759.

In addition to bricks, the Alexander account book records that rum was purchased for the men working on the Barrister's house. Between June 26 and July 28, 1759, over 38 gallons of rum were charged to Charles Carroll's account. The workmen were issued a daily ration of rum, and 38 gallons indicates that considerable construction activity was taking place. On July 14 alone, eight gallons were purchased.[1] Several times, specific men — Walkins, Rawlings, and Grimes Georghan—are noted as having made the purchases. These men were probably the heads of the crafts, such as the masons, carpenters and plasterers, working at the plantation, but surviving records do not indicate which building trades they plied.

By early 1760 the construction of the house and its dependencies was nearing completion. On the twenty-ninth of January Carroll wrote to Anderson to arrange for an indentured gardener, saying:

> There are often to be met with out of Business fellows that understand Common Gardening as Laying of Turf Kitchen and Flower Gardening mowing and the management of an orchard I am in want of such a one and would go as far as twenty Pounds sterling Crimp money Passage and all Expenses Included.

Later, in September, the Barrister sent a lengthy invoice to his agent which included a thermometer for the orangery, a copy of Miller's *Gardening Dictionary,* and the bowls and tacks for use on the bowling green. An orangery was an expensive luxury, and thus a status symbol in the eighteenth century. In addition to providing the family with the fruit from its trees, it visibly stamped its owner as among the very well-to-do. The only orangeries in Maryland believed to have been constructed earlier than Charles Carroll's were at Governor Sharpe's house in Annapolis and at Wye House in Talbot County, owned by Edward Lloyd, a cousin of the Barrister.

The same invoice included furnishings for the new house. Among them were:

One Turkey Carpet suitable for a Room 25 feet Long and twenty Broad at about Ten Guineas

one Ditto for a Room Twenty feet Long and Eighteen Broad at about six Guineas

two Looking Glasses with Gilt Frames of the Plain Genteel Fashion. The same Patterns for a Room thirteen feet Pitch with Double sconces or Branches fixed to the Frames of the Glasses as the Room where they are to Hang is stocco'd and no places left for fixing the sconces if separated from the Glasses at about Ten Guineas Each.

The Barrister was living in the new house by this time. On September 27 he wrote to his stepmother about her arrangements to return to Annapolis from Virginia, where she was visiting her nieces. Carroll explained that she would not be able to stay in the family's house on Green Street because a number of the servants were at his new residence. He went on to say, "I. . .Do not Keep House Constantly in Town being myself Generally at my House in Baltimore County."

Up to this time, the Carrolls had never referred to the property on which the new house stood by any particular name. The land records listed it as "Part of Georgia," its legal designation until the early nineteenth century. In their business papers, Dr. Carroll — and later his son — referred to their mills and shipyard "at Patapsco" and to the crops "at my Quarter at Patapsco." However, with the completion of the house and its grouping of outbuildings overlooking the terraced gardens, a more elegant name was needed. This was not just a house occasionally used by Charles Carroll on one of his plantations, but his country seat. He chose the name "Mount Clare" in honor of his sister Mary Clare Carroll Maccubbin and their grandmother Clare Dunn Carroll. After 1760 the Carrolls used this name for the estate, although occasionally they also referred to it simply as "the Mount."

Carroll had built on top of the foundations remaining from the earlier house, using their dimensions to determine the sizes of the parlor and dining room of the new one. To the north, the house was extended 14 feet to accommodate an entrance passage with the stairs to one side; opposite the stairs was a small room for the Barrister to use as a study.[2] This was a more sophisticated plan than one having a center passage containing the stair and running the depth of the house. With the least space lost to the passage, it provided convenient circulation among all the rooms. There could be a variety of room sizes with a large, well-lighted parlor on the garden side of the house. The plan still provided symmetry and a formal axis with a view from the entrance through the house to the garden in summer when the doors would be standing open.

This plan had already been used for several houses in Maryland. The John Brice II house in Annapolis, built circa 1730, is an early example. This same basic plan, sometimes with a small room between the stair and the front, would be increasingly used for important houses in Maryland until the end of the Colonial period.

The plan is also found in a number of the English pattern books which were imported into the colonies. These pattern books ranged from the small-sized *The Builder's Jewel*, by Batty Langley, which would fit into a carpenter's or joiner's pocket for handy reference on the job, to elegant folios such as *Vitruvius Britannicus*, by Colin Campbell, which would be found on gentlemen's bookshelves. The contents of the books ranged from the rules for proportions for

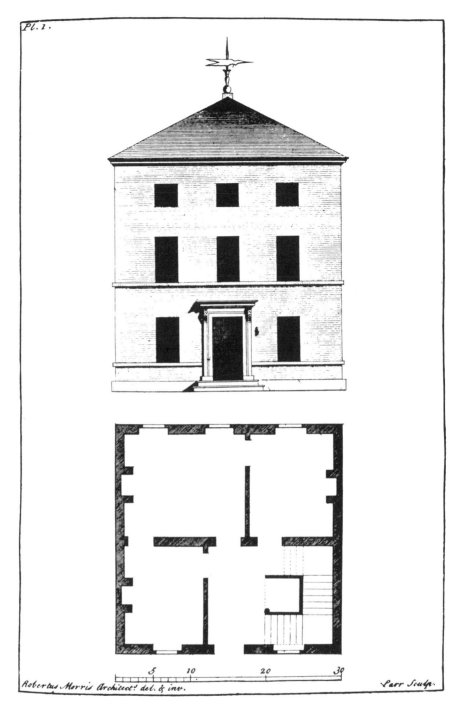

Plate I from *Select Architecture* by Robert Morris, published in London in 1755.

columns, methods of constructing staircases and roof trusses, details of mantlepieces and cornices, to plans for houses, churches, garden follies, and ornamental bridges.

Inventories of estates of planters and artisans indicate the wide ownership of pattern books. Advertisements by booksellers and the catalogues of lending libraries provide further evidence as to which books were available in Maryland in the eighteenth century.

One book which was widely used in the colonies and which contains the basic plan of Mount Clare on several plates is *Select Architecture* by Robert Morris. It was published in London in

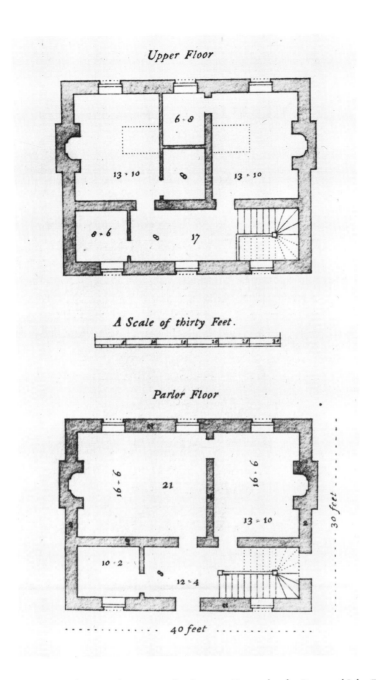

Upper Floor

A Scale of thirty Feet.

Parlor Floor

40 feet

ᏬᏇᏋ Plate II from *Twelve Designs for Country Houses* by the Reverend John Payne, published in Dublin in 1757.

1755, the year Charles Carroll returned from the Middle Temple, and is an exact reprint of *Rural Residences*, published by Morris in 1750.

Mount Clare's plan is also found in an Irish pattern book, *Twelve Designs*, by the Rev. John Payne, published in Dublin in 1757.

The entrance facade of the Barrister's new house had the stolid appearance of many mid-Georgian Tidewater houses. The 46-foot-long front was broken by only six openings with segmental brick arches. In the center, up two steps from the ground, a pair of paneled doors led into the entrance passage. To each side of the doors was a window, and across the front on the second floor were three windows. The roof cornice with molded brackets was the only ornamentation on this elevation.

Above a stepped water table, the wall was laid in an irregular Flemish bond; between each Flemish bond course of alternating headers and stretchers was a course of all stretchers. This unusual variation of Flemish bond is found on a number of houses in Yorkshire but has not been recorded as being used on any other building in Maryland.

The end walls of the house were laid in the same irregular Flemish bond. Each end had two chimneys built flush with the wall and continuing six feet above the roof. Below their brick capes, each had an ornamental band of stucco. Similar bands of stucco are found on many eighteenth century houses in the Chesapeake Bay region.

The east end of the house had only three windows, two on the second floor and one in the attic. These openings were constructed with segmental arches similar to those on the entrance front. At the ground level, by the base of the southeast chimney, was a bulkhead containing steps leading down to the basement.

Across the west end there were three windows on the first floor and three over them on the second. The attic contains one window centered under the gable and over the middle windows below. These openings had flat arches of rubbed and gauged brick.[3] The balanced position of the windows with their well-worked flat arches gave this side a more formal appearance than the opposite end.

The use of different types of arches over the windows in the end walls and the irregular Flemish bond coursing are two features of Mount Clare that have always interested architectural historians since they do not fall within any of the recognized Maryland building practices.

Looking at the west elevation, one can discern how the builder determined the depth of the new house. The two windows on this end which light the parlor are probably in the same locations as similar windows in the earlier story-and-a-half house. Using the center of the northwest parlor window as the center of the larger house, the builder extended the house 14 feet to the north. He planned a third window in the wall, lighting the study, to balance the southwest window in the parlor.

The severity of the entrance facade was in total contrast to the south or garden side of the house. Across this elevation are five openings on each floor. Again, a pair of paneled doors are in the center at the first floor. These doors opened out onto a wood platform with a flight of steps leading four feet down to the bowling green. The window and door openings are supported by flat arches of rubbed and gauged brick. At the eave, the modillioned cornice is the same as that on the entrance elevation.

This side of the house has a chamfered brick watertable, below which the wall is laid in correct Flemish bond. Above, it is laid in all header bond. This bond was used in other areas along the Eastern seaboard, but the greatest concentration of examples is found in the region centered around Annapolis.

Batty Langley, in his *London Prices of Bricklayers' Materials and Work*, published in 1748, described brickwork "when every course is laid with headers" as beautiful, although more costly than conventional bonding because it used more bricks and required more cutting and fitting by the masons. There are examples of all header bond in London, but its greatest regional use in England was in Dorset.[4]

The most distinctive features of the garden facade are its four giant brick pilasters. Sitting on bases projecting from the basement, they extend up the full height of the house to the roof line. The two center pilasters support a pediment which originally contained a bullseye window surrounded by rubbed and gauged brick with a keystone at the top.

This elevation of Mount Clare with its pilasters and center pediment is one of the most important expressions of English Baroque architecture in Maryland.

The use of giant pilasters and a pediment in the center of the most important facade of country houses was brought to England from Holland at the time of the Restoration. One of the first examples was Elton Lodge near London, designed by Hugh May in 1663. During the period of Sir Christopher Wren's influence, giant pilasters were used extensively on residences, churches and public buildings. Sir John Vanbrugh and Nicholas Hawksmore especially included them in the designs of their buildings.

The first house in Maryland known to have giant pilasters was Squirrel Neck, built by the Barrister's brother-in-law, Nicholas Maccubbin. In 1747, the year following his marriage to Mary Clare Carroll, Maccubbin purchased 740 acres on the Rhode River, seven miles below Annapolis in Anne Arundel County.[5] On the high land overlooking the river and the Chesapeake Bay, he built a five-part house, the center section of which was two-and-a-half stories high with a gambrel roof. At each end of the entrance and garden facades were two story brick pilasters with very simply molded brick capitals sitting under the wood cornice.[6]

The pilasters on Mount Clare are used as a stronger design element than are those on Squirrel Neck. The width of the shafts and detailing of glazed header bricks up the center of them are identical on Mount Clare and the Maccubbin house. The capitals on the pilasters at Mount Clare, however, are more technically advanced than those on the earlier house. Here they are composed of five courses of carefully molded brick. The brick bases are also better detailed than are those at Squirrel Neck.[7]

The cornices at both Mount Clare and the Maccubbins' house sit directly on the capitals of the pilasters. A classically correct entablature would have had a frieze and architrave between the capital and the cornice, but this evidently was beyond the knowledge or ability of both the Barrister's and his brother-in-law's builders. Because of the similarities in the two houses, in addition to the close relationship of the owners, it is likely that the same masons under the direction of the same master builder worked on both Squirrel Neck and Mount Clare.[8]

Although surviving records do not indicate who was responsible for the design and construction of the Barrister's house, it very probably was Patrick Creagh. Creagh was the most

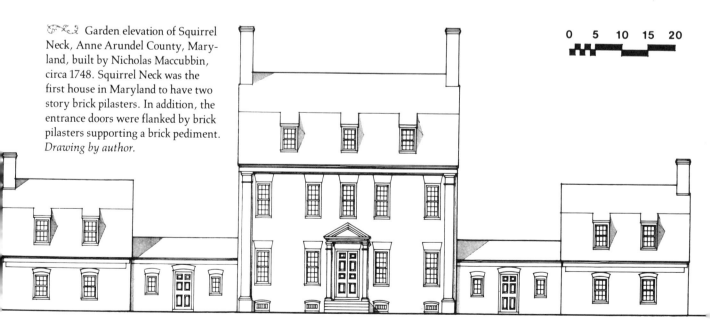

Garden elevation of Squirrel Neck, Anne Arundel County, Maryland, built by Nicholas Maccubbin, circa 1748. Squirrel Neck was the first house in Maryland to have two story brick pilasters. In addition, the entrance doors were flanked by brick pilasters supporting a brick pediment. *Drawing by author.*

0   5   10   15   20

prominent builder in Annapolis at the time Charles Carroll's house was under construction. In the 1740's, he had been responsible for the construction of the incompleted governor's residence, later dubbed Bladen's Folly. Patrick Creagh appears in Dr. Carroll's accounts several times during the same decade in connection with various building projects at the Georgia plantation. Creagh also owned the house and lots on Duke of Gloucester Street adjacent to the doctor's house on Green Street and he purchased the land adjacent to his own house on Prince George's Street from Dr. Carroll. Creagh's son, a ship's captain, carried cargoes for Dr. Carroll and the Barrister, and Creagh's son-in-law, Richard Maccubbin, was in the Barrister's employ in Annapolis at the time the new house was being built overlooking the Patapsco. With his prominence as a builder plus his connection with the Maccubbin family, Patrick Creagh may also have designed and built Squirrel Neck for Nicholas Maccubbin in the late 1740's. Creagh died suddenly at his plantation on the Severn across from Annapolis in December 1760, a date just following the completion of Mount Clare.

Whether the general ideas for the plans and elevations of Mount Clare came from the Barrister, from one of his friends who had a few architectural books, or from Patrick Creagh, if he were involved with the construction, the actual design of the plans and elevations would have been worked out by the builder or master mason. Until the end of the eighteenth century, the overall dimensions of buildings were set by a combination of geometric shapes and proportions. The more important the building, the greater the number of these shapes used. The proportions of Mount Clare's garden elevation show that it was designed by someone with knowledge and skill.

The garden facade is a square with the length of the house the same dimension as that from the ground to the top of the chimneys. Also, the length of the house is twice the dimension from

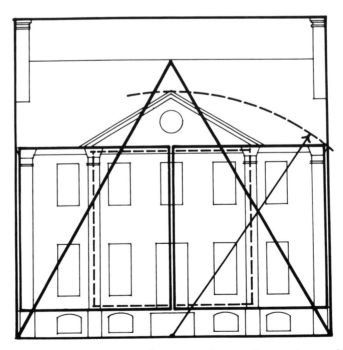

South elevation of Mount Clare, showing the gemetric shapes and proportions used to determine the dimensions of this facade of the house. *Drawing by author.*

the watertable to the eave, or two squares. (This was one of the most frequently used proportions in the Chesapeake region.) The top of an equilateral triangle whose base is the length of the house at the ground determined the top of the roof of the house. An arc with a radius from the centerline of the house at the ground to the corner of the house at the eave gave the height of the pediment. Another square is formed by the distance from the watertable to the eave equaling the dimension between the two pilasters supporting the pediment.

Within these overall proportions, the elevations were further developed using the width of the window opening as a unit of measure. The two principal elevations of the house are 14 units long and, from the watertable to the cornice, seven units high. There is half a unit from the watertable to the sills of the first floor windows, and the windows are two-and-a-half units tall. There are one-and-a-half units from the heads of the first floor window openings to the sills of the second floor windows. These windows are two units high. From the heads of the second floor windows to the bullseye window on the garden facade is another one-and-a-half units, and the diameter of the masonry opening of that window is one unit. Similar proportions of the windows and the vertical space between them are found on other mid-Georgian houses in the Chesapeake Tidewater region.

The entrance facade illustrates how the designer or master mason used the same unit of measure to locate the windows. Here, there are two-and-a-half units between the center window and those flanking it and three units between those windows and the corners. This slightly greater dimension between the windows and the corners gives a rhythm to the wall and makes the corners appear stronger.

The house, when completed in 1760, had only one adjacent dependency — a one story kitchen on its east side. The 22 by 24 foot kitchen may have been constructed by Dr. Carroll at the time he built the original house because the south end of the building aligned with the front wall of the earlier house. This relationship of a house to its dependencies was one of the standard arrangements in the eighteenth century in both Great Britain and her colonies. It is thought that if his younger son had lived, the doctor would have balanced the kitchen dependency with another to the west of the house for use as an estate office.[9]

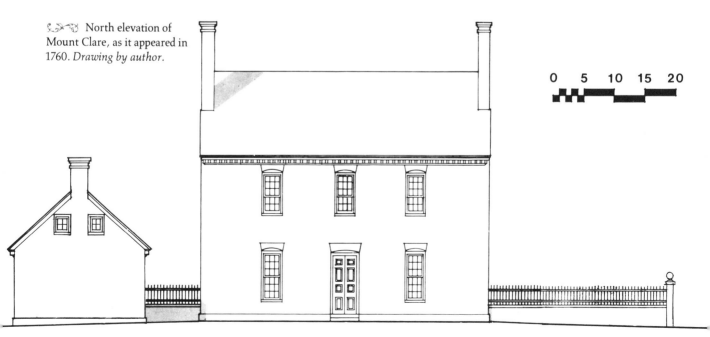

〔※〕 North elevation of Mount Clare, as it appeared in 1760. *Drawing by author.*

0   5   10   15   20

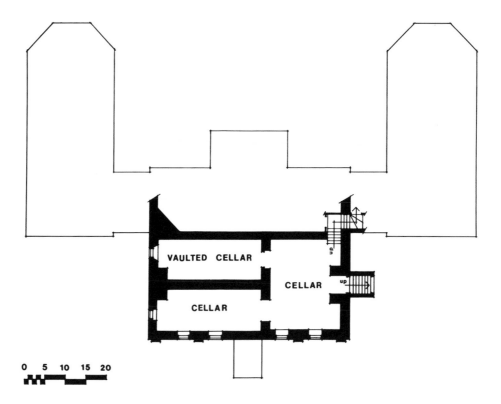

Basement plan of Mount Clare, as it appeared in 1770. The basement dates from the one-and-a-half story house built by Dr. Charles Carroll in 1750. When the Barrister built the present house in 1757, the brick partition between the three cellers was doubled in thickness to support the increased weight of the two-and-a-half story structure. The interior stair from the basement to the east hyphen was added at the time the hyphen was constructed in 1768. *Drawing by author.*

The Barrister, evidently, neither felt the need of a separate office when he built his new house, nor did he feel that the entrance front of the house needed the symmetry of a balancing outbuilding. The garden elevation was the only one that it was thought required a balanced composition. The fact that a dependency was not planned to be built at the west side of the house may explain why the window heads on that end were constructed with the more expensive flat arches that were used on the garden facade.

The kitchen building was connected to the house by a low brick wall topped with wood palings. Similar dwarf brick walls with palings extended west from the house and forward to form a rectangular forecourt. In the center of the north side of the enclosing "palaissade", on axis with the entrance doors of the house, were gate posts surmounted by lead lions. Inside the forecourt was the carriage circle and on the outside, service lanes led to the outbuildings on each side of the house.

The lead heraldic beasts were ordered from William Perkins, a London merchant. The Barrister wrote Perkins in the summer of 1757, "I received safe the Goods shipped in the *Betsy*," but his letterbook does not contain a copy of the invoice which he must have sent with one of the several letters to the merchant the previous fall. Seven years later, Charles Carroll wrote to Perkins in great irritation to say that he had tried to pay for the goods by shipping iron to him, but that Perkins's ship captains would not "Consign you any Effect I Deal in." Carroll closed the matter by sending a bill of exchange for £32.0.6 sterling for the lions, noting that would leave only one shilling ten pence unpaid.

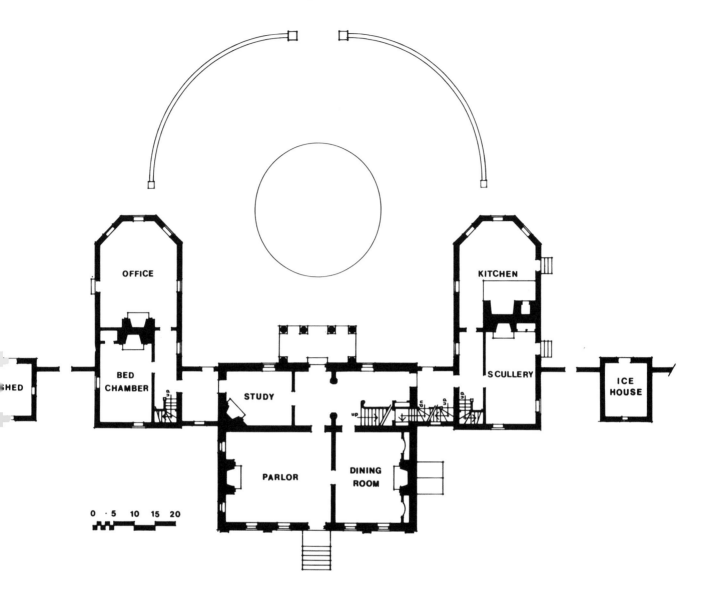

OFFICE

KITCHEN

BED
CHAMBER

STUDY

SCULLERY

SHED

ICE
HOUSE

PARLOR

DINING
ROOM

0 · 5   10   15   20

First floor plan of Mount Clare, as it appeared in 1770 after the completion of the alterations designed in 1767 and constructed the following year. The locations of the windows and doors in the east and west walls of the wings and the locations of the staircases in the wings are conjectural, but based upon mid-eighteenth century examples in the Chesapeake Tidewater region. *Drawing by author.*

In contrast to the enclosed forecourt on the north, on the garden side the composition of the house and its dependencies stretched along the length of the bowling green. Beyond the kitchen was a 27 foot square laundry building. Balancing it on the west was an orangery, or "greenhouse" as they were termed until the middle of the nineteenth century. These outbuildings were hip roofed, each with a chimney rising from the center of its roof. The two buildings rose up 30 feet to the tops of their chimneys, giving emphasis to each end of the 240-foot-long range of buildings. Grass ramps led down from the bowling green to a series of garden terraces of "falls," as they were always called in Maryland. Beyond the falls, pastures and fields stretched to the river three-fourths of a mile away.

The basement of the Barrister's house, dating from the earlier house built by his father, extends only under the parlor and dining room. The walls are stone for the lower three feet and brick above. A brick lateral wall, built to brace the long walls of the original basement, was doubled in thickness to support the thicker brick walls of the new two-and-a-half story house. The location of this existing wall was used to determine the sizes of the parlor and dining room above.

The portion of the basement under the parlor is divided into two cellars, the one on the north side having a brick barrel vault supported by the stone walls. The opening to the vaulted cellar was altered early in the twentieth century, but the doorway to the adjacent area is intact with its wood lintel dating from 1750 and a segmental brick arch in the portion added in the late 1750's.

The floor in the basement is laid with two shapes of bricks. The south cellar under the parlor has square brick pavers which are believed to date from the Barrister's lifetime. The remainder of the basement floor is laid in rectangular brick set in a herringbone pattern. These probably were put down to replace square pavers worn by much use. The only entrance to the basement was through the relieving arch under the southeast chimney. Outside, the steps down from the lawn were protected from the weather by a bulkhead.

On the first floor, all the walls except those in the study are fully paneled. The baseboards, chair rails, door and window casings, and the panels below the window seats—all of which would receive hard wear and knocks—are wood. The large fielded panels and the cornices are plaster. Similar plaster paneling is found in a number of houses in Annapolis and its surrounding region and is considered to be another of the Annapolis characteristics of the middle Georgian period. Belair, in Prince George's County, built for former Governor Samuel Ogle in the 1740's, retains plaster paneling in its entrance passage. This plasterwork, generally considered to be the earliest surviving plaster paneling in Maryland, is very similar to the paneling in Mount Clare.

The use of plaster instead of wood for wall paneling is also found in a few English houses and a larger number of Irish ones of the same period. It is believed that plaster was used as a fireproofing measure. Since the paneling was always painted, the casual observer would not realize that it was not wood.[10]

The short entrance passage at Mount Clare leads through to the parlor on the garden side of the house and to the 12 by 16 foot study to the right of the passage. The study has plain plastered walls with a molded chair rail and a cornice. There was a window in the end wall near the corner fireplace and another which looked into the forecourt.

To the left of the passage, through an arched opening, is the staircase. The molded arch with a carved keystone is supported by a pair of triple-cluster pilasters. These fluted pilasters with Roman Doric capitals and bases sit on short pedestals half the height of the chair rail. This arched opening with its surrounding woodwork, set in a paneled wall and surmounted by a cornice, is the richest decorative element to survive in the house from its period of completion in 1760.

The four foot wide stair rises in three runs to the floor above. Its molded mahogany hand rail is supported by fluted balusters. At the first floor the hand rail ends in a full "twist" supported by a group of four balusters acting as a newel. The ends of the treads are decorated with simply cut brackets. At each landing, the hand rail is ramped with a double curve.

The hand rails on the stairs of a few other eighteenth century Maryland houses have similar ramps at their landings; there are also examples in England and Ireland. One Irish example, 33 Molesworth Street, Dublin, built 15 to 20 years earlier than Mount Clare, has a plastered paneled staircase as well as a similar hand rail. The hand rail at Hampden in Talbot County, dating from the early eighteenth century, is ramped with a double curve, and the newel at the first floor is a cluster of balusters.

The parlor and dining room at Mount Clare occupy the entire garden side of the house. The 20 by 25 foot parlor is the largest room on the first floor and was well lighted by a window at each side of the fireplace and two overlooking the lawn. There are also double doors leading out to the bowling green. These doors are centered on the long facade and are on axis with the door leading to the passage and the pair of entrance doors. The window openings in the parlor, as they do typically throughout the house, extend below the level of the chair rail to form window seats. The wall panels under the window seats are wood rather than plaster because of the kicks and knocks they could be expected to receive.

The dining room, measuring 16 by 20 feet, has two windows on the garden side and doors opening into the parlor and the stair passage. A pair of arched headed cupboards recessed into the paneled wall flank the fireplace. Behind pairs of paneled doors in the arched openings of the cupboards are curved shelves for storing china and glass. Such pairs of cupboards were still a relatively new design concept at the time of the house's construction since a separate room for dining only developed in the middle of the eighteenth century. As late as 1776, the inventory of Governor Eden's recently completed house in Annapolis did not list a dining room or "eating parlor", as they were often called at first.

Shortly after the American Revolution, the original materials in the first floor rooms were removed and new ones installed, so that today there are no indications of the designs of the originals.

During the second half of the nineteenth century, the jambs and heads of the window openings were also altered. Originally they must have been similar to the paneled jambs and heads of the door openings leading to the lawn and the entrance. Very likely, paneled shutters folded back into the window jambs.

It is possible that William Brown, who was responsible for the interior woodwork in Dr. Upton Scott's house in Annapolis in the mid-1760's, might also have made the woodwork for Mount Clare. In concept and detailing, the work in the two houses is related. William Brown was a joiner and cabinetmaker with a flourishing practice in the Annapolis region from the mid-1740's until his death in the late 1790's. His shop was in Londontown on the South River in Anne Arundel County, where he also operated an inn and ran the Lower Ferry. At the time the

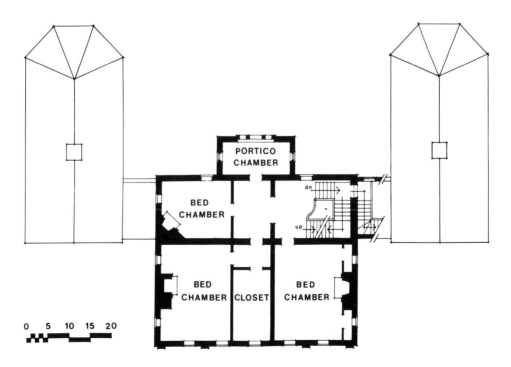

Second floor plan of Mount Clare, as it appeared in 1770. *Drawing by author.*

23

Barrister's house was under construction, there were no other houses in or near Baltimore of comparable quality, and there may not have been a joiner locally available to design and produce work such as the pilasters and arch between the entrance passage and the staircase. The overall concept and construction of Mount Clare make it an Annapolis regional house, and whoever was responsible for its building would very naturally have used craftsmen he knew in Annapolis or nearby. If the original mantels in the parlor, dining room, and study had survived, a more positive attribution to Brown perhaps could be made.

The second floor plan basically repeats that of the first floor. The area surrounding the stair is the only one to have plaster paneling on the walls. The other rooms and passages on this floor have flat plastered walls with chair rails and cornices.

To the left of the stair, over the dining room, is a bed chamber with two windows overlooking the gardens. On either side of its fireplace is a shallow closet. Each is lighted by a window, and their short end walls have rows of pegs for hanging clothes.

Through a wide arch, the stair landing opens into a passage, the size of the entrance passage below it. Originally this space had a window located over the front door and looked down onto the carriage circle.

Beyond the passage, and above the study, is a small bed chamber with a corner fireplace. The mantel in this room, one of the two in the house which date from the house's completion in 1760, is a simple rectangle with a molding around its outer edge. The bottom of the horizontal member over the fireplace opening is enlivened by a pair of ogee curves separated by a molded keystone.

Over the parlor was the Barrister's bed chamber. The space is divided into what was then an unusual arrangement in a Maryland house, but one with which the Barrister would have been familiar through his years in England. Off the passage is a small lobby. This leads both into a bed chamber, well lighted by four windows, and into a dressing room. This latter room would have been known as a "closet" in the eighteenth century and used not only for dressing, but also for bathing and for storing the Barrister's linen and clothing.

The mantel in the Barrister's bed chamber is the other surviving original one. It is also basically a simple rectangle with a molded outer edge. At the two corners and at the floor, this mantel breaks out in crossettes or "knees." When originally installed, the surrounds inside these two original mantels would probably have been plastered, and the fireplaces would have had brick hearths.

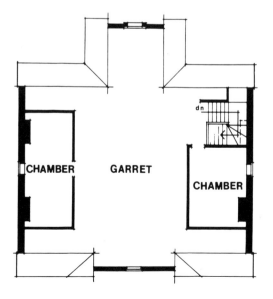

 Attic plan of Mount Clare, as it appeared in 1770. The chambers at either end of the attic were servants' bed chambers. *Drawing by author.*

CHAMBER   GARRET

CHAMBER

dn

0   5   10   15   20

The staircase with its molded hand rail and turned balusters continues in two runs up to the attic. Along the east wall, above the landing between the two runs of steps, the brickwork for the northeast chimney swells out from the wall. This is a false chimney which never contained flues and was built only for external balance.

At each end of the attic is a finished room with plastered walls and ceiling and a window centered under the gable. These rooms were used as servants' bed chambers. The remainder of the attic is an open space with the roof framing exposed. This area, or garret, was used for storage and was lighted by the bullseye window in the pediment on the garden elevation.

With a residence in Annapolis for the winter and a seat in the country for the summer, the Barrister settled down to enjoy the pleasant life of a very well-to-do bachelor. He continued ordering his clothes from Jonathan Reynolds, the tailor he used when living in London. His servants were dressed in green livery trimmed with scarlet, which also came from England. He enjoyed racing. His fishing tackle and shot for duck shooting were ordered from England. One invoice to Anderson included two dozen wine glasses, four one-quart decanters, four one-pint decanters, a two-quart silver tankard and two silver pint cans.

In July 1760, as Mount Clare was nearing completion, Charles Carroll ordered a curricle, the sports roadster of his day, from the merchants Capel and Osgood Hanbury in London:

> I desire you will send me by the first opportunity Convenient to Annapolis one Good strong Light Carricle with Harness for two Horses with the Inclosed Coat of Arms or Crest as fashionable on the Carricle. the Wheels I would not have over High as our Roads are not the best. it must not be heavy as will not suit Getting into our Ferry Boats or small Horses. of the Genteel Taste but not whimsical and one strong Leather Portmanteau Trunk to Carry a suit or two of Cloths and some shirts with straps to fasten behind the Carricle such as they usually Travel with behind Post Chaise with a Couple of Good Light Whips for Driving.

Each year the parish records of St. Anne's in Annapolis, where Charles Carroll was a communicant, listed him among those taxed for remaining a bachelor. As the wealthiest one in the province, the Barrister must have been considered a catch by many parents with marriageable daughters.

In the summer of 1763 he finally changed his status when, on the twenty-third of June, he married his 21-year-old-cousin, Margaret Tilghman. The June 30 issue of the *Maryland Gazette* announced: "Thursday last CHARLES CARROLL Esq; (Barrister) of this City was Married in *Talbot* County to Miss MARGARET TILGHMAN, (Daughter of Matthew Tilghman Esq;) a young Lady of great Merit, Beauty and Fortune."

The Tilghmans were descended from Dr. Richard Tilghman, who had arrived in Maryland in 1659 and settled in Talbot County at a plantation he called The Hermitage.[11] Matthew Tilghman, a grandson of the doctor, was raised at The Hermitage. When his cousin, Matthew Tilghman Ward, died in 1741, he inherited his cousin's very considerable estate. The same year he married Ann Lloyd, a first cousin. They made their home at Bay Side (now known as Rich Neck Manor), one of the plantations Tilghman had just inherited, at the mouth of the Miles River and the Chesapeake Bay in Talbot County. Both Matthew Tilghman and Ann Lloyd were first cousins of Dorothy Blake, the Barrister's mother.

Margaret Tilghman, in addition to marrying a man with one of the largest incomes in the province, was wealthy in her own right. When she was four years old, her great-aunt, Mrs. Margaret Bennett Ward, died leaving her over £4,000.[12]

Both the Tilghmans and the Carrolls were pleased with the marriage. Richard Tilghman II, of The Hermitage, when writing to a cousin in England in the fall of 1763, added the postscript: "My brother Matthews oldest daughter Margaret was laterly married to Charles Carroll Esqr of an agreeable person and fine fortune."

The Andersons in London (Mrs. Anderson was related to both the bride and the groom) sent congratulations to the newlyweds. The Barrister replied, writing: "Peggy joins me in Returning you and our Cousins sincere thanks for your Kind wishes and Compliments." He also sent a long invoice with such articles for the new Mrs. Carroll as:

one full Dressed Ladies Suit of Cloths of Rich white Ground Brocade if Can be got and fashionable with a slight Gold Sprig or flower interspersed / send in a yard of the same to spare

A Suitable Laced Head Dress and Ruffles and Handkerchief &c of Lace about two Guineas p yard / a shade or thin mantle

A Suitable Stomacher and Bows and a pair of Shoes,

and also

one Fashionable Ladies Gold watch Chased with a Chain and Equipage Suitable,

and

1 Light stone or Paste Necklase or Solitaire which is most fashionable about 5 or 6 Guineas

Toward the end of the invoice, the bridegroom requested "The Best Book of Cooking Published."

With the signing of the Treaty of Paris in February 1763 ending the French and Indian War, England's colonies entered a new period of prosperity. The Barrister's invoices to Anderson in London reflect the increasing wealth of Margaret and Charles Carroll and the style of living they enjoyed. On the second of October 1764, the following list was sent:

58 yards of Substantial Silk and worsted Crimson Damask for window Curtains for a Dining Room @ about 8/ per yard and one hundred and Sixty Eight yards of Proper Binding of same Colour

29 yards of Green worsted Damask for Curtains for a Common Parlour

84 yards of Proper Binding of the same Colour

2 neat Mahogany Chest of Drawers

6 Carpet Bottom Mahogany framed Chairs about 15/ per for Bed Chamber

6 Strong Ditto about Ditto Black Leather Bottoms for a Parlour. And two Arm Chairs of the same Sort.

A Large Easy Arm Chair well Stuffed in the seat Back and Sides Covered with Common Stuff Damask and a Cushion

A pair of End Irons Brass Knobbed with a fire shovel and Tongs and pair of Bellows for a Bed Chamber made Strong

2 pieces 24 yards in Each of Cotton for a Bed & Curtains of a white Ground and Lively Colours

one Silver Bread server or waiter to suit a small Company about 8 or 10 Persons fashionable Light and Handy I have seen them in the fashion of Fruit Baskets or Sea Shells

one Black Shagreen Case with a Dozen Silver Handled Table Knives and Forks and one Dozen Spoons

one Ditto Case with a Dozen Silver Handled Desert Knives and Forks and a Dozen Desert or Custard spoons

one Plain Silver three Pint Chocolate Pot

one Cream Pot of middle size I suppose the Fashion to be Chased

one small Silver waiter about 10 ounces.

my Crest or the same Coat as was Cut for Peggys Seal to be put on the Plate or if the Coat be Lost put mine

Sir William Temples works 4 vol[s] Octavo

Lord Shaftsburys works in four vol[s] Containing his Letters

Lord Molesworths History of Denmark

And Bishop Robinsons Account of Sweden

Polnitys Memoirs

Keatings History of Ireland or the best Irish History Published

about 20/ of the Best Political & other pamphlets yearly Especially those that Relate to the Colonies

4 pair of Crimson Silk and worsted Damask window Curtains for 4 Large windows two Curtains to a window Each Curtain two Breadths side and 2½ yards and three Inches in Length

2 pair of Ditto Curtain for two End windows of the same Length with only

a Breadth and Half in Each all Lined with thin Durants or Lammy of same Colour as may be necessary as our suns may spoil them.

2 pair of Green worsted Damask window Curtains for two Large Parlour windows Each Curtain two Breadths wide and two yards and a Half and three Inches Long.

One Single Ditto Curtain two Breadths wide and same Length with former for an End window these Green worsted I think need not be Laced all the Curtains to be Properly bound Round with Binding of same Colour and to be Quilled at Top

These Articles wrote for instead of the Stuff and materials for window Curtains Mentioned in the beginning of this Invoice

Two days later Carroll wrote again with another invoice:

7 lb Green Tea @ 14/ per

2 lb Hysen Ditto @ 18/ per

7 Loaves of Double refined Sugar

7 Ditto of Single Ditto

Mace 4 ounces

Cinamon 6 ounces

Nutmegs 4 ounces

Cloves 4 ounces

one womans Hunting Saddle of the Large Easy Sort of Green Cloth with a Strong but narrow Gold Binding or Trimming on the Cover and proper Furniture wth Bridle Suitable

2 Wicker Baskets Lined with Tin one open Down the Sides for Carrying Clean Plates the other Close for fowl and one for Knives

12 Packs of Playing Cards

3 Dozen Bottles of Fresh Pyrmont water in Quart Bottles or what they call Half Bottles

3 Dozen fresh German Spaw water

1 lb best Jesuit Bark Powdered and Close Packed

2 Gallons Best Lamp Spirit for Tea Kettle in pint Bottles well Stopped

1 Dozen best shaving wash Balls not much perfumed

Silk and Cotton Binding for the two Pieces Cotton wrote for, for Bed and Curtains

one Plain green Silk waistcoat for myself of Corded Green Silk not made too Short. Eccleston has my Measure.

Set of Table China as follows viz.
2 Large enamald China Dishes
4 Ditto a Size Less
2 Ditto the next Size
4 Ditto of the Least
1 Middling Sized Soup Dish
3 Dozen enamald Plates to suit the Dishes
2 Dozen Soup Ditto
2 Sallad Dishes

2 Bowls or Pudding Dishes

6 Saucers or shells for Pickles

1 Dozen Nankeen Bread and Butter or Breakfast Plates

1 Dozen very fine Damask Napkins

2 7/4 Damask Table Cloths

6 8/4 Diaper Table Cloths

6 6/4 Ditto Ditto

1 piece of Course White Dowlass

1 folio family Bible Red or blue Cover Strong Paper Gilt

2 Prayer Books Blue Covers Gilt in octavo

1 piece of Brocade with white ground in Lively Colours that will Cost about 15/ per yard made up in a negligee and Coat or any other Garment if more fashionable

1 piece of point Lace Lappits

a Silk and Gold Flounce to Trim the Coat and Side of a French Robe

3⅜ yards broad Silk and Gold nett Lace

10 yards of narrow Ditto

1 piece 8 or 10 yards fine Cotton Stamp'd with Lively Colours

1 piece fine Lawn

2 Gause Caps. 8 yards of Rich flowered Gause

6 pair womens best Kid Gloves. 6 pair Ditto mitts

4 pair Ditto fine India Cotton Hose

2 pair Ditto thread Ditto

3m best midling pins and 3m short white Ditto

3m Lilykin Ditto[13]

The curtains were still a problem because in the letter accompanying the second invoice, the Barrister wrote: "We think it Better to have the Crimson Silk and worsted Damask and the Green worsted Damask window curtains made up with you so have this Article altered from the first Invoice sent and wrote for the Curtains instead of the Stuff and materials." One suspects that the "We" was Mrs. Carroll.

At about this time, Charles Carroll began interesting himself in the career of Charles Willson Peale, a saddle maker in Annapolis who had ambitions to become a painter. In July of 1764 the Barrister wrote to "Mr. Twinihoe, Attorney at Law" in London inquiring whether Peale had inherited an interest in his grandfather's estate, Wotton Manor in Oxfordshire. In describing Peale, Carroll said, "The young fellows Circumstances are but Low."

Two years later the Barrister was one of several patrons in Annapolis who contributed to a purse to enable Peale to study in England. In addition, Carroll wrote to his agent on October 29, 1766, between ordering grass seed and clothing from Eccleston, his London tailor, saying:

I have wrote to you by a young man of our Town one Charles Wilson Peale and Desired you would advance him on my Account a sum not Exceeding in the whole Twenty or Twenty five Guineas as my motive is Purely to Enable him to put Himself into some method of Gaining a Little Insight into the Profession of Limning and Painting which he seems to have a Turn for I hope he will make a Good use of it.

It was hoped by Peale's backers that he would "have staid at least two years in England." So upon hearing from Peale the next year that he might soon return to Maryland, the Barrister penned a letter of advice to the young painter:

Mr Peale

It was a Pleasure to me to find by yours of the 17th March last that you were in a way of Acquiring some Improvement in your Profession but I was a Little surprized to her from Mr Anderson that you had thoughts of Leaving England to sail for Maryland the November following the Dates of your letters as I supposed you would make your stay in England as Long as Possible to Git all the Insight you Could and as I Calculated the Assistance you Carried from Hence would enable you to make a Longer stay but I hope both Mr Anderson and myself were mistaken and that you have Conducted yourself with that Prudence and Frugality that you will not have occasion to hurry away before you have in some measure attained the Ends for which you went. You are to Consider that you will never be able to make up to your self and family the Loss of the opportunity and that those by whom you have been Assisted will be sorry to find their money Thrown away but I hope as I before said that I have been mistaken and those hints are unnecessary. I have wrote to Mr Anderson and left it to his Descretion in Case he should judge you Deserving to advance you Eight or Ten Guineas more on my Account.

I observe your Inclination Leads you much to Painting in miniature I would have you Consider whether that may be so advantageous to you here or whether it may suit so much with the Taste of the People with us as Larger Portrait Painting which I think would be a Branch of the Profession that would Turn out to Greater Profit here you Likewise mention the Copying of Good Painting by which I suppose you mean the Study of History Painting. This I look upon as the most Difficult Part of the Profession and Requires the utmost Genius in the artist few arrive at a High Point of Perfection in it and indeed in this Part of the World few have a Taste for it and very few Can go thro' the Expence of Giving that Encouragement that such an artist would Desire but after all Consult and be guided by the best of your own Genius and Study that Branch to which your Disposition Leads you and that you Judge most suitable to your Talents you had better be a Good Painter in Miniature than Indifferent one in Either of the other Branches and be Assured that what I have above wrote and mentioned Proceeds from my Desire of your welfare As I am

Your Friend and Servant

Cha. Carroll

Annapolis October 29th 1767
To Mr. Charles Wilson Peale
to the Care of Mr Wm Anderson

Charles Carroll was always positive in knowing what he wanted. In one of his earliest letters to Anderson, he stated:

I . . . desire you would by the first of your ships Coming with Convoy Convenient to Annapolis send me the Contents of the Inclosed Invoice and make Insurance thereon so that in Case of Loss I may Recover the amount of them Clear of all Charges as they are for my own use I would have them the best of the sorts — the furniture of the neat Plain fasshion and Calculated for Lasting nothing of the Whimsical or Chinese Tast which I abominate.

Although they may have ordered their furnishings to be in a "neat plain fasshion," the Carrolls also wanted them to be in the current taste. In September 1768 they sent for:

1 Fashionable Genteel Large Silver Waiter or Salver Seventeen or Eighteen Inches in Diameter or over, not thick Chased all over but a Genteel Light Sprig Round only and Coat of Arms in Middle

one Plain Ditto about Eight or Nine Inches in Diameter or over This must be Cup or Pillar footed as it is for the Middle of a Table

4 D° half Pint Cocoa nut shaped Drinking Cups Cup footed without Handles Gold Gilt Insides

Coat of Arms or Crest on all Plate

and in the accompanying letter, the Barrister gave more details:

The Large waiter I write for she Calculates will Hold Eight or Ten Tea Cups and Saucers and is for a Tea Waiter. The small one is to stand in the middle of a Table to support a Dish as the Cross or X Lamps do not suit well must have a Genteel Cup or Pillar of Like the Glass stands used for Deserts. The Cups are for Drinking small Beer or Rhenish. Glasses are Continually Breaking.

Their invoices show that the Carrolls were among the few families in America at that time who used rugs on their floors, both at Mount Clare and their house in Annapolis. In addition, in the spring of 1767 they ordered:

2 Good Painted floor Cloths, one of them to be 18 feet Long by 16 feet wide the other 16 feet wide by 12 feet Long, both made of the best and strongest Duck and Painted so as to bear mopping over with a wet mop and Put up Dry and so as not to be Cracked or to have the Paint Rubbed of.

Along with the invoice, the Barrister wrote, "My wife would have some slight woolen Rolled up with the floor cloths to Prevent their Rubbing so as to be Defaced by Getting the Paint off, if any Danger without it." From their sizes, they evidently were intended for use at Mount Clare.

All the goods shipped to the Carrolls had to clear through the port of Annapolis, but not everything arrived at their dock there as ordered. The blades of a dozen ivory-handled knives were rusted because they had not been oiled, two expensive four foot long red leather trunks trimmed with brass nails arrived shattered, several gallon size square bottles in an oak case were broken— and, what was worse, their contents of "best old French Brandy" were lost.

By the second half of the decade, the Carrolls, along with other propertied families in Maryland, were enjoying the greatest period of prosperity the province had known. The Governor, Horatio Sharpe, was well liked and an able administrator. Taxes in Maryland were lighter than those in the neighboring colonies. There were ready markets for the products shipped to England. A steady influx of settlers were buying and developing farms on the western lands which had been taken up by the Dulanys and Carrolls and other land speculators a generation before.

With the increased wealth and luxury came increased building activity, which in turn encouraged the arrival of new craftsmen trained in the current English styles. These men brought with them more highly sophisticated architectural knowledge than had been previously available to Marylanders.

Throughout their lives the Barrister and his wife showed an awareness of style changes, and with the generous means at their disposal they were able to remain constantly in the latest mode. In 1766, Mount Clare was less than ten years old, but its simple, conservative entrance front began to look old-fashioned to the Carrolls. Thus they decided it was time to think about modernizing their country house.

Silver tea canisters in Chinoiserie design with Japanned chest. The canisters are engraved with the Carrolls' amorial device. Height of canisters 5⅞ and 5½ inches, made by Samuel Taylor, London, 1760-61.
Collection of the Maryland Historical Society; gift of Miss Clare Goldsborough Holliday.
From the invoice sent to William Anderson, the Barrister's agent in London, in September 1760:
> 1 Shagreen or other Fashionable Tea Chest with silver Furniture with two silver Tea Canisters and a sugar Canister or Dish neatly Chased or Carved about thirteen pounds

and from the letter dated September 30, 1760 that accompanied the invoice:
> Pray my Compliments to my young Lady Cousins and Tell them that I Desire their Taste in my Tea Chest it is a piece of Peculiarly Lady's Furniture and it will not be Inconsistent with the Nicest Delivery to Grant this Favour to a Batchellor so many Leagues Distant from them and a Relation besides. Nay if they would Amuse themselves A morning in Directing any thing Else they think within their Province the Exercise might Contribute to their Health or at Least to their Healths being Drank in this Province

Landscape showing the south, or garden front, of Mount Clare by Charles Willson Peale. On April 11, 1775, Peale wrote to Charles Carroll, Barrister, "I have been at work on your other Landscape & I hope to have it ready for the figures by next week, when I shall send them to Annapolis with Mrs. Peale". In the foreground is the Barrister and a companion (thought to be his brother-in-law, Nicholas Maccubbin), accompanied by a groom in the Carroll livery. Beyond the pasture and a snake rail fence are the series of "falls" with flower gardens leading up to the house. On either side of the falling gardens are orchards and vegetable gardens. The whereabouts of the companion painting, presumably of the entrance front, is unknown. *Private collection.*

III

THE HOUSE
1767-1783

The decade preceding the Revolution was one of brilliant building activity throughout Britain's American colonies, and it was during this period that Annapolis was transformed into the social and fashion capital of the Chesapeake Bay country. In 1769 Thomas Eddis, arriving in the suite of Robert Eden, the new governor, wrote of Annapolis:

> It is . . . the seat of Government; the public offices are here established; and as many of the principal families have chosen this place for their residence, there are few towns of the same size in any part of the British dominions that can boast a more polished society. . . . In the vicinity of Annapolis are many pleasant villas, whose proprietors are eminent for their hospitality.

The first great Annapolis house of the era was Dr. Upton Scott's, begun about 1762, followed by John Ridout's in 1765. The Ridout house sat above the harbor on Duke of Gloucester Street, and its garden adjoined Charles Carroll, Barrister's. At the same time, on the other side of the Severn River, Governor Sharpe was building his retreat, Whitehall, and across Roberts Creek (now College Creek), Thomas Sprigg's new house, Strawberry Hill, overlooked the city from above its terraced garden.

Observing these new, high-style residences being constructed around them, the Carrolls were determined to alter their country house to bring it into current architectural taste. During the winter of 1766-67 the plans for the changes to Mount Clare were prepared, and that February the Barrister wrote to William Anderson in London for hardware for the additional doors and for one hundred weight of white lead.

In the summer, Carroll sent for more materials for the house. On July 2, 1767 he wrote to the merchant firm Sedgley, Hilhouse and Randolph in Bristol:

Gentlemen:

I shall Ship you in the first of your Ships that arrive here Bar and Pig Iron that will Amount in Value to about one hundred and thirty Pounds Sterling Fifty Pounds of which I shall take out in Iron ware and other Coarse Goods from you Part of the Remainder for I hope it will not take near the whole of what will be Left I Intend to apply to Executing the Plan Inclosed that is Purchasing the Round Columns and those to which the Pilasters Join The Stone, and marble mentioned in it I do not Know the Cost of such mentioned but I suppose the stone must Come Cheaper from the Quarries near Bath than Else where as it is Easily Hewn and the water Carriage to Bristol Convenient and the Black and white Marble I suppose will be Equally Reasonable. The Plan is for a Portico or Colonade to be Joined to the Front of a House and Project Eight Feet from it, An Arch at Both Ends, for a Passage through it, to Spring from Pilasters of Stone Joined to the End Pillars of the front of the Portico and the two three Quarter Round Columns, I think they Call them, that Run up Close to the wall of the House; The manner of which may be Easily seen and the hight of the four Round Columns in Front and the two others by a work man in the Ground Plan and the Profile or side View which I send you Inclosed.

The Columns must be Round of the Plain Doric order and the Proportions Exact according to the scale and Plans in Length and Diameter, And those to which the Pilasters are to be Joined in one, and as I Conceive Hewn out of the same Block or Blocks, that make up the Columns, and with the Columns, must be Cut Exactly in the manner that may be Easily Discovered by a workman Inspecting the Plan as the full Round Columns and those with the Pilasters Joined to them will be Composed of Different Blocks or Pieces of Stone to be Placed one upon the other Putty or Cement for Joining must be sent in with them or Instructions How to make it. The Stone and Marble must be Carefully Packed and the Captain Instructed to have them Gently Lowered onto the Hold or the Cases may be Broken and the Stone Broken or Defaced.

Every thing I think so plain that an Artist Can not mistake on Casting his Eye on the Plan if any Doubt However, Let me Know by the very first opportunity or if the Cost of what is mentioned in the Plan far Exceeds the Remainder that will be in your Hands After Purchasing the fifty Pounds worth of Goods I shall write for, tho' as I before mentioned I hope it will not amount to so much. I send you this to Give the more time to have what I mention Ready to send by your first ship next year. I shall write to you by the Ship I send my Iron in and in the mean time am

Gentlemen your Most H^{ble} Servant:

Chas Carroll

The next month he wrote again to the same firm:

Gent.

By the first of your Ships Coming in to Annapolis I Desire you will send me the Contents of the Inclosed Invoice and the Stone and Marble mentioned in mind of the 2^d July Last according to the Directions of the Letter and Plan Inclosed in it in Case the Cost be Reasonable as in the Letter mentioned.

I need not I hope Desire the Greatest Exactness in the Stone Cutter and Person of whom you Git the stone and marble as they must be sensible that the Least Deviation, Mistake, or variance from the Plan Can not be Remedied here and must Render the whole that will be sent useless to me

Let all sent be Insured in such manner that in Case of Loss I may Draw my Principal and Charges

I am Gentlemen y^r M H^{ble} Servant:

C. Carroll

Annapolis Maryland
August 6th 1767
To Messrs Sedgley Hilhouse and Randolph
Merch^t in Bristol[1]

The additions to Mount Clare transformed the simple entrance front into a Palladian villa composition. This stylish architectural concept for country houses — that of a villa element flanked by wings terminating in pavilions — had spread through England in the 1750's. New houses were designed and older ones altered to conform to this new ideal. Along the Thames at Twickenham and Roehampton and Richmond, aristocratic and merchant families alike built villas as weekend retreats from London. Wrotham Park in Middlesex, designed by Isaac Ware in 1754 for Admiral John Byng, through its influence on both patrons and architects, was perhaps the most significant house designed in the Anglo-Palladian villa concept in that decade.

The leaders of Colonial society quickly adopted the new Palladian style. The Redwood Library in Newport, Rhode Island, designed by Peter Harrison in 1749, is an early example. The Tidewater planters' desire to build in this new mode was typified in Mount Airy, built by John Tayloe, near Warsaw, Virginia, at the same time that the changes to Mount Clare were being constructed.

When the alterations to Mount Clare were completed, the north elevation appeared as a new, unified composition. One now came up the quarter-mile long lane from the public road and, passing between gate piers surmounted with the lead heraldic beasts, entered the redesigned forecourt. The old walls had been demolished and new, curved brick walls topped with palings built in their stead. The new walls connected the gate piers to the wings of the house and enclosed a semicircular space. A west wing had been constructed, connected to the house by a hyphen. The kitchen building had been lengthened to match the new wing, and a hyphen built to connect it too with the house. The north ends of the wings were semi-octagonal in shape to give the impression of pavilions. In the center of the house, a portico or piazza, with a chamber above it, was added to give distinction to the earlier, simple elevation and to provide a needed focal point to the entire composition of the entrance front.

This highly three-dimensional composition was in contrast to the long, two-dimensioned garden side, just as the new Palladian aspect of the entrance was in contrast with the earlier English Baroque feeling of the garden elevation.

The composition of the north side with its outreaching forecourt walls, the long wings to each side of the house, and the portico which projected forward from the house was one of the most expressive examples of "movement" in eighteenth century Maryland architecture. This feeling was heightened by the transitions from the low, curved palisades to the one story wings and then up to the two-and-a-half story house with its forward thrusting, vertical element of portico and chamber.

Robert Adam in his preface to Volume I of the *Works in Architecture of Robert and John Adam* in 1773 best defined "movement," saying:

Movement is meant to express the rise and fall, the advance and recess with other diversity of form, in the different parts of a building, so as to add greatly to the picturesque of the composition. . . . That is they serve to produce an agreeable and diversified contour, that groups and contrasts like a picture, and creates a variety of light and shade, which gives great spirit, beauty and effect to the composition.

The two wings were 22 feet wide and 50 feet long. They extended forward from the front of the house 36 feet forming a "courtyard" as one contemporary writer described the space. Each wing contained two rooms divided by a center chimney and a narrow passage. In the east wing, a new kitchen was built to the north of the existing one. The old kitchen became a scullery and was reduced in size by the addition of a passage connecting the new kitchen with the hyphen. The west wing contained the Barrister's office. Behind it was a chamber for his clerk and a passage.

Whoever designed the alterations to Mount Clare was familiar with current English architectural trends. With an ingenious eye and a sense of style, he totally revolutionized the appearance of the entrance front. In the process, he introduced several stylish design ideas to Maryland.

The semi-octagonal ends on the two wings were the first such in the province. The designer could have known of this idea from contemporary English examples. In addition, the concept was illustrated in several pattern books, including two known to be in use in Maryland at the time: Isaac Ware's *A Complete Body of Architecture* and *Select Architecture* by Robert Morris.

The semi-octagonal ends of the wings at Mount Clare created pleasantly shaped spaces at the north ends of the new kitchen and office, and the three windows in each end provided more light, but the overriding reason for their use was the desire to terminate the wings in a highly fashionable shape.

The hyphens connecting the house to the kitchen and office wings would have been a great convenience to the Carrolls and their servants. Under the staircase, a door was cut through for

North elevation of Mount Clare, as it appeared in 1770. A comparison of this elevation with its earlier appearance shows the transformation of the stolid and conservative house into a high-style Anglo-Palladian villa. *Drawing by author.*

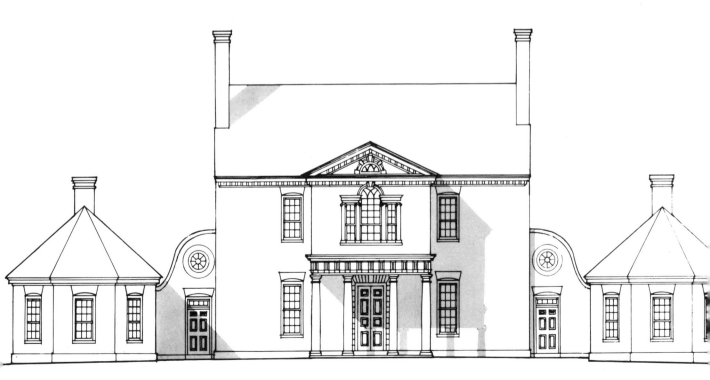

access to the east hyphen and the west window in the Barrister's study was lengthened to make a door leading to the other one. Each hyphen also had a door leading into the forecourt.

An unusual feature of the hyphens was the ogee shape of the tops of their walls. The ogee curves served as transitions from the one story wings to the taller house, as well as leading the eye toward the visually dominant center element, the portico. The curved walls were needed not only for visual reasons; the east one, at least, was also practical. The ogee curve provided head room for the back stairs that ran from the first floor of the hyphen up to the second landing of the stair in the house. A door cut through the wall provided access from the landing to the service stair. A circular window over the door from the hyphen to the forecourt provided light for the new stair.

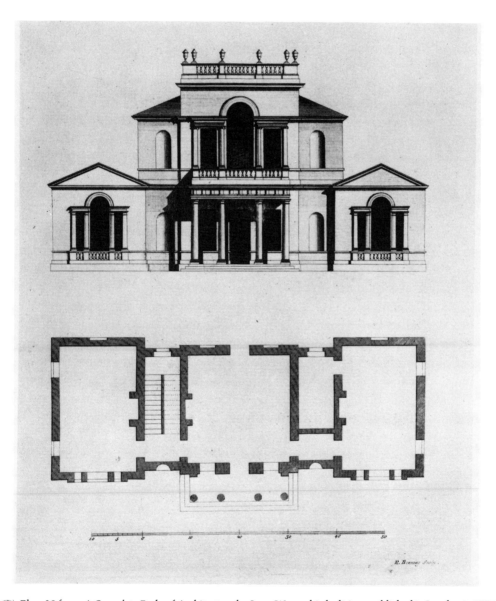

✎ Plate 39 from *A Complete Body of Architecture* by Issac Ware, third edition, published in London in 1756. This plate illustrates a Venetian window with ionic pilasters over a porch with Roman Doric columns. Of all the illustrations in the pattern-books known to have been used in the colonies, this plate is the closest example to the center pavillion on Mount Clare. *Courtesy of the Henry Francis du Pont Winterthur Museum Library.*

The concept of back stairs was introduced to England from the Continent in the late seventeenth century and came into general use in Great Britain during the eighteenth century. The service stair at Mount Clare — permitting the servants to go from the work areas to the second floor without passing through the first floor of the main house—is the earliest known to exist in a Maryland house.

The ogee curve on the west hyphen was constructed only for balance, and the circular window in its north elevation was a false window, again for balance. The curved walls on the hyphens were repeated in reverse shape on the roofs of two small outbuildings standing between the office wing and the orangery on one side and between the kitchen wing and the laundry on the other. These one story, brick buildings had curved hip roofs terminating in carved finials. From references to a deep, brick-lined pit under it, the 12 by 14 foot outbuilding on the east is believed to have been the ice house. The use for the balancing one on the west is unknown. These two buildings with their elegant roofs are thought to have been constructed at the same time that the Barrister and his wife were making the changes to Mount Clare in the late 1760's.

The most important change to the house was the addition of the portico with the chamber above it. The eighteen foot wide portico projects eight feet from the face of the house. Up one step from the forecourt, four stone columns across the front and two semi-engaged columns against the house support the chamber above. The carefully cut columns with their Roman Doric capitals and bases, and the marble paving composed of alternating blocks of gray and white, were sent in response to Charles Carroll's letters to Sedgley, Hilhouse and Randolph in the summer of 1767. The columns are of a limestone known as Bath stone because of its great use in that city in the eighteenth century.

The face of the house between the semi-engaged columns is stuccoed with rustication around the entrance doors. The rusticated door surround gives an added element of architectural sophistication to the composition of the entrance front and made the entrance doors the ultimate focal point of the axial composition that began as one came up the long driveway and passed between the gate piers into the forecourt.

The stone columns of the portico support a wood Doric entablature above which are brick walls carefully laid in Flemish bond. On each side wall is a small window set in a masonry opening with a segmental brich arch. The north elevation of the second floor of the pavilion contains a Palladian window, which was known as a "Venetian" window in the eighteenth century. This Venetian window at Mount Clare was the second on a Maryland house, the first being on John Ridout's in Annapolis. Between the three glass sections are Ionic pilasters supporting entablatures from which springs a molded arch with a rusticated keystone. The proportions of the Venetian window as well as the details of the woodwork surrounding it follow those given for similar windows in the pattern books. William Halfpenny's *Practical Architecture*, which went through five editions between the beginning of the eighteenth century and 1736, illustrated a number of Venetian windows. The window at Mount Clare follows the dimensions for the example in Plate 48, about which Halfpenny wrote: "The following Window was originall from the Venetians but is here represented with its Proportions as used by ye Modern Architects."

The arch and its keystone project into the cornice of the pedimented gable of the pavilion. Set in the pediment above the cornice is a semi-circular window within a rusticated frame. The details of this window and its surround are identical to those in the pediment on the entrance facade of Dr. Upton Scott's house on Shipwright Street in Annapolis.

The high quality of the woodwork on the north elevation of the center pavilion and its close relationship to work on Dr. Scott's house make a strong argument that the joiner William Brown was responsible for its execution.

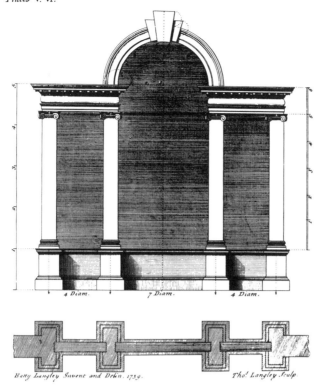

Figure LIII from *The City and Country Builder's and Worker's Treasury of Designs* by Batty Langly, third edition, published in London in 1750. An illustration of a Venetian window of the Ionic order very similar to those on the John Ridout house and Mount Clare. The book went through a number of editions and was widely used in both Great Britain and America.

The chamber above the portico at Mount Clare was a small but very stylish room. The door leading into it was made by lengthening the existing window in the upstairs passage. The room was flooded with light from the Venetian window, which takes up most of the north wall, as well as from the small windows in each end. The cornice, door and window casings are similar to those on the rest of the second floor. There is no chair rail in order to emphasize the "pedestals" under each window. Here the walls break forward an inch with the window sills forming the tops of the pedestals, and the baseboards acting as the bases. The molded baseboards are the most elaborate in the house.

The middle of the eighteenth century saw the development in England of the use of a small second floor room as a boudoir. The *Oxford English Dictionary* describes the eighteenth century use of "boudoir" as a private sitting room, usually upstairs, where the mistress of the house could read or write or entertain close friends. No doubt this is how Mrs. Carroll used the portico chamber. Since Mount Clare was used as a summer residence, the lack of a fireplace was not important while the excellent cross ventilation and the north light through the Venetian window must have made the room pleasant on hot summer afternoons. Mrs. Carroll's boudoir at Mount Clare was among the very first examples in Maryland of a room designed for this use.

Mount Clare's elegant two story pavilion was very much in the Anglo-Palladian tradition of using a projecting, decorative, center element as a focal point to contrast with the relative simplicity of the general mass of a house. It was also in the regional Tidewater tradition of placing a porch with a chamber above it at the entrance of a house or a public building. This familiar feature on Tudor and Jacobean buildings was brought to America with the early colonists, and continued in use longer in the Chesapeake Bay region than it did in either the northern colonies or in England.

Architectural evidence indicates that several houses in Jamestown had porches with chambers over them. Malvern Hill in Henrico County, constructed in the 1660's, is another early Virginia example. Bond Castle, built in Calvert County in the late seventeenth century, was one of the earliest documented Maryland examples.

At the time the alterations to Mount Clare were designed, two important Annapolis buildings with which both the Barrister and his architect would have been familiar had this holdover feature. The State House, which dated from 1705, had a porch with a chamber over it. The design of the building was based on an earlier State House that had stood on the same site in State Circle, and that in turn, had been based on the 1676 State House at St. Mary's City—both of which had had porches with chambers.[2]

The other example familiar to the Barrister would have been the house of Daniel Dulany the Elder. Later used as the Superintendent's residence at the Naval Academy, and demolished in 1901 to make way for Bancroft Hall, it was one of the outstanding houses in Annapolis. Sometime before the middle of the 1750's, Daniel Dulany extended his original house and added a porch with a chamber above it to visually unify the long facade.

The portico and its chamber at Mount Clare were the most sophisticated in design in this long tradition of use in Maryland and Virginia. The Barrister's architect, while seeing the holdover use of Jacobean porches in Annapolis and the Chesapeake region, also approached the design problem of a center focal element using his knowledge of fashionable English architectural ideas.

From the beginning of the Jacobean period on, loggias, three bays wide with a room above, had been constructed as focal points in English gardens. Although used for out-of-doors dining or as studies or bath houses, these two story pavilions were designed more for their elegant external appearance than as useful buildings and usually made use of the stylish classical architectural vocabulary.

The garden house, built about 1727, at Widcombe Manor on the outskirts of Bath, which used Roman Doric columns to support the chamber over the loggia, was well known to the visitors to that resort in the eighteenth century.

Another example with design elements found also on Mount Clare is the pavilion at the end of the canal in the garden of Bodnant in Denbighshire. A Venetian window lights the chamber over the loggia, and above the window is a pediment enriched with sculpture. The pavilion is capped with a roof of the same shape as those on the two small outbuildings at Mount Clare. This elegant garden house at Bodnant was originally built in a garden in Gloucestershire in the 1730's and was moved to its present location 45 years ago.

Elements in a number of plates in the architectural books used in England and America illustrate portions of the center pavilion on Mount Clare. Plate LVIII in James Gibbs's *A Book of Architecture Containing Designs of Buildings and Ornaments*, published in 1728, shows a country house with an advancing center element containing a piazza or loggia with a chamber above and a pedimented gable. Thomas Lightoler's *The Gentleman and Farmer's Architect*, published in 1764, shows on plate 6 a two story house with one window on each side of the advancing center pavilion, as at Mount Clare. The plate also shows a Venetian window on the second floor of the center pavilion over the entrance door and a semi-circular window in the pedimented gable over the Venetian window. Plate 9 in this same volume shows a five part house with semi-octagonal ends on the wings.

Of all the books known to have been in use in the colonies, plate 39 of Isaac Ware's *A Complete Body of Architecture,* published in 1736 and reprinted in 1760 and 1764, contains the closest example to the center element at Mount Clare. The center section of the house illustrated on plate 39 contains a porch with Roman Doric columns supporting a Doric entablature over which is a Venetian window. James Brice of Annapolis owned a copy of this book at the time the changes to the Carrolls' house were being designed. Later, Charles Willson Peale used this same plate for the villa in the background of his group portrait of Edward Lloyd IV of Wye with his wife and daughter, painted in 1771.[3]

A direct influence on the design of the center pavilion on Mount Clare was the garden elevation of the Ridout House on Duke of Gloucester Street in Annapolis. The Carrolls must have watched this house being built, just beyond the garden of their town house, when they were in Annapolis. In the center of the first floor of the Ridout house is a porch with Roman Doric columns and Doric entablature supporting a pedimented roof. Above the porch roof at the second floor is a large Venetian window with Ionic pilasters. When the house was constructed, a brick and wood balustrade ran across the facade above the cornice at the attic level. A brick pediment broke the balustrade in the center of the elevation with the arched head of the center section of the Venetian window projecting into the pediment. This enabled the arched section to light the attic. At the time John Ridout's house was completed, its garden elevation was the most sophisticated and architecturally advanced composition within the city of Annapolis.

Garden elevation of the Ridout house, Annapolis, Maryland, built by John Ridout, circa 1765. This drawing shows the balustrade which originally sat above the cornice on the garden and street elevations. *Drawing by author.*

When Charles Carroll, Barrister, wrote to Sedgley, Hilhouse and Randolph in the summer of 1767, he indicated that he was enclosing a drawing of the stone columns and paving. Unfortunately, there is not a copy of the drawing among the Barrister's papers, nor did he mention the name of the architect who designed the alterations to Mount Clare.

Of the houses in the Annapolis region constructed in the mid-1760's, the one which most closely exhibits the same high style Palladianism as Mount Clare is the John Ridout house. As with Mount Clare, there are no surviving documents among the Ridout family papers indicating who the designer of their house might have been. Equally disappointing for the architectural historian is the lack of building records of the Upton Scott house and the original portion of Governor Sharpe's elegant villa, Whitehall.

The additions at Mount Clare show the work of an architect with an eye for style, one with recent knowledge of English architectural trends, and a person who delighted in being ingenious.[4] The same characteristics mark the design of the Ridout house. In addition, the closeness of time between the construction of the two projects and the proximity of their owners make it more than probable that the same architect was responsible for both the Carrolls' and the Ridouts' houses. To this same unknown person, the designs of the Scott house and Whitehall perhaps could also be attributed. All of the owners were members of the province's aristocracy and three of them were among the inner nucleus of the "court party."

Between the death of Patrick Creagh in 1760 and the earliest documented reference to the architect Joseph Horatio Anderson in April 1771, there are no records of anyone in the Annapolis area with the talent to design a formal building.[5] Some day, it can be hoped, an account book or a diary or a packet of letters will be unearthed to give flesh to the forgotten architect.

Center pavillion on the entrance facade of Mount Clare. *Drawing by author.*

The columns and paving for the portico for Mount Clare would have arrived in 1768 and that summer must have seen the construction of the projecting entrance pavilion. Looking ahead to the following year when the alterations would be completed, the Barrister, in July of 1768, wrote to his agent in London about a housekeeper:

> we are in want of Sober orderly woman of a Good Character that understands Cooking Pickling Preserving and the other Requisites for a House keeper if Elderly we shall Like her the Better. I suppose such are to be met with that would on moderate wages I suppose about Ten or Twelve Pounds Sterling per Annum Come to a Good Place Here for some years we shall be much obliged if such a one to be Got that you would agree with Her for us on the best Terms and send her to us if above the ordinary Rank of servants my wife will Like her Better, as she will meet with all kind Treatment But she must not be of the flirting kind or one that give herself airs.

At this same time, the invoices in Charles Carroll's letter books illustrate the continually increasing scale of living his wife and he were enjoying. In the Spring of 1768 Mr. and Mrs. John Morton Jordon sailed from Annapolis for England and carried the following list to Mr. Jordon's firm of Jordon and Maxwell in London:

> one Diamong Hoop Ring—Mrs Jordon has the Size—but it is desired to be Rather Less and the Sparks as Large as Can be Got for about 15 Guineas.

> two other Hoop Rings such as Mrs Jordon shall Chuse, the two not Exceeding two or three Guineas—and a small size less than the Diamond.

> one Handsome Mahogany Cabinet with best furniture and Locks of Different Sorts to the Drawers and Doors, and if any Carved ornament to the mouldings they are Desired to be solid and not Glued on such work being very apt to Come to pieces here.

> one piece Rich black Sattin made into a Robe or negligee and to the Inclosed body Lining with Genteel Trimming

> two pair of Table Bottle stands with Silver Rimes, with Crest or Coat as Inclosed.

In July of the same year the Reverend David Love, rector of All Hallows Parish in Anne Arundel County, returned to England for a visit and carried this invoice to the Carrolls' usual agents, William and James Anderson:

1 Piece of fine Irish Linen @ 5/

1 piece fine Ditto @ 4/

1 piece of fine Cambrick

1 piece Good Strong Napkening Diaper of a Middling Size

3 pieces of Dowlass

2 pieces of the Best osnabrigs ⅞ wide

2 lb. best whited Brown thread

12 lb. best osnabrigs D°

6 lb. of Coloured D°

6 pair of mens Large Strong thread stockings

3 pair of Boys D°

4 lb best Hyson and 10 lb best Green Tea

14 Loaves best Double and 14 Loaves single refined sugar

4 ounces Cinnimon

¼ hundred best Ship Bisquit

½ hundred best Spanish Whiting

1 Furkin best Split Peas

6 two Quart Bottles to be filled 2 of them with Capers two with anchovies one with olives and 1 wth best Salad Oil

one Dozen small Enamelled thick old China Cawdle or Chocolate Basins with Saucers to them

2 Coffee Pots of best Burnt or Enamelled China to hold about a Pint

2 China Pint Cans

} These are Desired to be very Good and Well Chosen

3 Dozen Wine Glasses
2 Wine and Water Glasses
2 Quart Decanters
2 Pint Ditto
} To suit a Glass Sent

1 Salver or Something Proper to Raise a Middle Dish on Table of Either Glass or China, Rather China

4 Mustard Glasses Like the broken one sent

2 best flint Square Quart Bottles Ground Stopers and narrow mouths

4 best flint Pint Ditto for a Case to be made Here

1 Lawn or Gause Search* of the finest and best Sort with Leather Top and Bottom

6 Hair Sifter Bottoms of the Twilled sort that are fine and Good

2 very Good Box Irons with Hammered Heaters

1 best Tin fish Kettle about 2 feet or 26 Inches Long

6 best Larding Pins Different sizes

A set of Tagging Irons for Cutting and Marking Paste

one Egg Slice

2 best Sugar boxes and Mallets

2 Jack Spits one of the a Good Size for Joints of Meat the other for small fowls with Handles Ready fixed for Chain.

1 Neat Suit of Blown Lace head Cloths which must Either have Handkerchief or Typet to it to Cost about four or five Pounds.

1 worked Muslin Apron of the Clear Sort worked in Sprigs with an Edge Round it.

1 Suit of Fashionable Ribbon

1 Fashionable Gause Cap

1 Breast flower

12 Yards of an Edging Commonly Called Jacobs Ladder for the Tops of Lawn Aprons

1 Genteel set Sprig for wearing in the Hair of Paste and opal mixed

* intended for "Searce," a fine sieve

16 yards of fine bright Blue Mantua Silk or Lutestring

1 piece of India Persian of blue or Pink Colour which Can be Got the brightest and not too Deep it must be very Good and not Gumed

1 Tunic white Callico Quilted Coat of the wove kind

8 pair of fine Grain Kid Gloves

4 pair of Ditto mitts

1 pair of Fashionable Silk mitts

6 pair of fine India Cotton Hose

4 pair worsted Ditto — Those sent last year to Coarse

2 pair Silk Shoes one pair Plain the other Embroidered

6 pair Fine Callimancos with fine worsted bindings

1 pair Good Clogs with the Straps Covered wth strong silk To be made to the Measures Sent by the same Hand that made the silk Shoes Last year — not master Hose but George Stagg I think his name is

1 piece of Striped Duffill for Blanketing

1 piece of Cloth coloured Kersey with Trimmings

2 pieces of blue Half thick

1 Dozen mens best felt Hats

1 Dozen Ditto ordinary

1 Light mans beaver of same Size of that sent me last year ab^t 18/

1 Dozen mens Double worsted Caps

1 Dozen womens large blue yarn Hose

6 pair of Mens silk Stckings for Myself 3 pair of them to be white silk and 3 pair of them to be of the fashionable mixed Colour.

The Reviews for 1768 and those omitted to be sent me Last for 1767

About twenty shillings best Pamphlets

The Act of Parliament to Explain amendment and Reduce into one Act the Several Statutes now in being for the Amendment and Preservation of the Public High ways in England it was Passed I believe in 1766 or 1765

4 Gallons Port wine in Quart Bottles

4 Gallons Ditto in Pints D°

6 Gallons best Rhenish wine in Pint Bottles

4 Gallons Battavia Anock in Quart Bottles

6 Gross best Velvet Corks

¼ Chest best Lisbon Lemons by your first Ship and ¼ Chest by your Last

10 m 10ᵈ and 5 m 20ᵈ nails

4 Good S pipe Stock Locks at 4/each

6 Good S pipe and Pad locks

50 lb of Drop and 50 lb of small mold shot Size about the Bristol Drop

2 Dozen blue and White Check Handerchiefs

2 pieces Check Linen

1 piece Grey fearnought

1 piece Green Livery Cloth with Red Shalloon for Lining and Red Mohair—

½ Gross brass Buttons Coat and ½ Gross D° Vest—

1 piece of Ticking or Coarse Trustain such as they make Servants Frocks of and 6 Skains Red Mohair

½ Gross flat yellow Metal Coat Buttons well shanked

1 Good seine forty Fathom Long Vest twine and strongest well Corked and Leaded

A Set of Strong and Good Harness for four Horses to Drive Post Chariot Fashion two Postilion Saddles with Crest on the Brass Plates on the off Horses—

9 yards of strong Gold Lace for Housing or Saddle Cloths of the Inclosed Pattern

As much Good Crimson Broad Cloth as will Make me a waistcoat and Good strong narrow Gold Lace with Lining of

the same Colour and Proper Trimmings Buttons to Button to the Bottom

½ Dozen Bottles best orange Shrub well Corked and Directions how to make Shrub—if they Can be Got from the Makers—

A Bushel of Rocques Burnt seed one ounce of finest Cantaleup melion seed

one ounce Romand D°

2 voilet Pardigon	⎫	
2 Moroco	⎬	Plumb Trees
2 Sᵗ Catherine	⎭	
4 orange	⎫	
4 Turkey	⎬	Apricot Trees
4 Brida	⎭	
4 Roman	⎫	
6 Newington	⎬	Nectarines Trees
6 Roman	⎭	
3 Hereforshire Heart	⎫	Cherry Trees
3 Carnation	⎭	
2 East Sᵗ Germain	⎫	
2 Skinless		
2 Pound Perkinsons warden		
2 Dry martin		Pear Trees on
2 Autumn Burgamot	⎬	Tree Stocks
2 Supreme		for Standards
2 Largonelle		
2 Royale	⎭	

NB: I would have all the above Trees 3 years old from the Graft or Bud if Can be safely moved or as old as they Can be moved—

1½ lbs best Glauber Salts

1 piece Green Cotton

25 lb. Brimstone.

6 lb of Salt Petree

4 Boxes of wafers

2 Dozen Sticks best Red Sealing Wax

½ Dozen Sticks black D°

2 Gross Empty Quart Bottles

2 Round Long Haired wall Brooms

6 Large Mop heads

6 Best Curry Combs without Brushes

1 Dozen wash Balls

1 Ream of ordinary uncut writing Paper	2 Dozen Pewter Basins for a Dairy to hold a Gallon Each
24 Quire best Large Post Paper	

On December fifteenth the Barrister wrote to the Andersons amending his order written the previous summer:

Dr Sirs/

By Captain McLachlan you will Receive Nineteen Tons of Bar and Eleven Tons of Pig Iron and a Certificate of the same being Plantation made. I have not as usual Inclosed the Certificate to you but sent it to Mr Lloyd to Give to him as I think Love told my Clerk that it was necessary to show it to the officers at Clearing out the Vessel.[6]

My wife in our Invoice of the 21st of July wrote for Sixteen yards of blue mantua Silk or Lutestring if these Reaches you time Enough, make the Quantity nineteen yards. She also in Her Letter to her Cousin Desired that the woman we wrote for should understand something of Clear Starching and Serving But as we want her Principally for a Housekeeper her understanding Cooking Pickling &c will be more Material. So that if it be Dificult to meet with one that may understand the Clear Starching and at the same time the Cooking &c. She Desires you will not Let that be any objection but send her a Good orderly Cleanly woman that will do for the Managing Her Kitchen and Housekeeping.

Our Streets are bad for Carriages at Night Desire you will send me in half a Dozen Links such as Footmen Carry behind Coaches, our Compliments attend all with you

I am Dr Sir your M h^{ble} Servant
Charles Carroll

The wide range of articles included in the Carroll invoices illustrates the difficulties wealthy Americans experienced trying to live fashionably and comfortably in the eighteenth century. The comments in the letters accompanying the invoices reflect the frustrations of trans-Atlantic shopping which must have been further aggravated by the six to twelve month wait between sending the order and the arrival of the goods. In September 1760 the Barrister wrote Anderson:

Dear Sir

Yours of the 5th Last march with the Goods per Montgomery Came safe to hand Every thing to please Except the China Tea ware which I think both ordinary and Dear at six Guineas besides being bad of the kind very full of flaws and Blemishes such as I suppose the shop keeper Could not Dispose of at Home

As many of the things I now write for are Expensive Require Nicety and must be Lasting Please to give your Tradesmen Directions to be Exact and Carefull

The quality of the tea they received was a constant irritation to the Carrolls and provoked a series of comments starting October 1764 with: "The Tea Indeed Peggy Does not think the best for the Price." The following October, the Barrister was more specific:

My wife still makes Complaint about her Tea that sent Mr Tilghman is Indeed Extraordinary Good which She has been used to But this of ours has no more flavour than a Chip Pray Let the Alderman Know that we have Tho' out of the sound of Bow a Distinguishing faculty in our Tastes and for the future Let us have his best with his Paper and Name on the Cannisters.

Two years later, although the tea merchant had risen in the world, Mrs. Carroll did not think the quality of his tea had improved. In a letter of October 29, 1767 to his London agents, the Barrister first delivered his wife's complaints about the poor fit of the shoes Mr. Hose made for her and continued saying:

My Compliments Likewise in a Particular manner to the Good Knight Alderman and Grocer Sr Thomas Rawlinson and Let Him Know that Imposing upon a man is by no means a Deed of Chivalry if he Does not mend his manners tell him and send me Better Tea I shall think the Touch of his Majestys Sword has no more Virtue than the Imposition of Hands of a Bishop it Gives only a Little Pride and Leaves the morals and Principles of a man just where it found them.

Finally, in July the following year, he wrote:

The Tea you sent us in this year from Messrs Rawlinson and Company is very Good Pray make my Compliments to them and Desire we may always have the same.

Books were always important to the Carrolls. Dr. Carroll's letters and invoices to his London agent often included lists of books to be sent to him. In a letter to his son before the young man left the Middle Temple, the doctor had reminded him to "bring a Good Collection of Necessary Books." Later, the Barrister constantly added to the library he inherited from his father. His letters and invoices frequently contained requests for books and pamphlets to be sent from England.

While the quality of the tea upset his wife, the Barrister's ire was raised by the bookseller. In 1764 he wrote to Anderson:

I shall be obliged if you' Direct your book seller (I hope he is a man of Taste) to send me in yearly about 15 or 20 shillings of the Best Political and other Pamphlets Especially any that Relate to the Interest and Circumstances of the Colonies or the monthly Reviews but none of Religious Controversy it is some Amusement to Learn from your authors and their works of wit how things Pass with you he may forward them as opportunity offers.

Four years later he told his agent:

My master Strahan has Charged me with two vol^s of Reviews for 1767 and has not sent them another Pamphlet Published in 1766 he has sent me with a Pin altered the Date of 1768 I have it not here at the mount now or I would Inclose it to him Pray tell him that I Expect the Reviews. Besides the Cur has no Taste in his Choice of Pamphlets Let him Know unless I am better served shall apply to some other Book Seller.

The gardens were an important and integral part of Mount Clare from the very beginning of the Barrister's planning. By 1760, when the house was first completed, the bowling green and falls had been laid out and the orangery constructed, and after Margaret Tilghman Carroll became the mistress of Mount Clare in 1763, the scope of the gardens was increased. From the edge of the bowling green, the hillside dropped forty feet in a series of falls laid out in flower gardens. At their centers, on axis with the center of the house, were grass ramps connecting the 300 foot long falls. The two upper levels were divided at each end by smaller terraces at their half levels. To each side of the falls were vegetable gardens, and beyond them were orchards. In late October 1770 Mrs. Mary Ambler, from Jamestown, Virginia visited Mount Clare and described the gardens in her diary:

About two Miles from Baltimore Tn is an exceeding Handsome Seat called Mount Clare belonging to Mr Charles Carrel of Annapolis Son of Dr Carrel this Seat is withinn Sight of the Baltimore Iron Works & when M Ambler was at that Place the Beauty of Mr Carrels Seat tempted her to take a nearer View of it & she Walked there on Satury Afternoon with Mrs Brook & took a great deal of Pleasure in looking at the Bowling Green & also at the Garden which is a very large Falling Garden there is a Green House with a good many Orange & Lemon

Detail of landscape by Charles Willson Peale showing the south, or garden, front of Mount Clare. 1775. Oil on canvas. *Private collection.*

Trees just ready to bear besides which he is now buildg a Pinery where the Gardr expects to raise about an 100 Pine Apples a Year He expects to Ripen some next Sumer, the House where this Gentn & his Lady reside in the Sumer stands upon a very High Hill & has a fine View of Petapsico River You Step out of the Door into the Bowlg Green from which the Garden Falls & when You stand on the Top of it there is such an Unifomity of Each side that the whole Plantn seems to be laid out like a Garden there is also a Handsome Court Yard on the other Side of the House. This Gentn is one of the Proprietors of the Baltimore Iron Works He has no Child.[8]

A view of Mount Clare painted by Charles Willson Peale in 1775 shows the gardens and the house with its connected dependencies stretched along the hilltop. When John Adams was attending the Continental Congress in Baltimore in February 1777, he strolled with Elbridge Gerry down a point of land called Ferry Branch. Looking across the Patapsco River, Adams saw Mount Clare and in his diary described the view much as Peale had painted it:

Took a walk with Mr. Gerry, down to a Place called Ferry Branch, a Point of Land which is formed by a Branch of the Patapsco on one Side and the Basin before the Town of Baltimore on the other. At the Point is a Ferry, over to the Road which goes to Annapolis. This is a very pretty Walk. At the Point you have a full view of the elegant, splendid Seat of Mr. Carroll Barrister. It is a large and elegant House. It stands fronting looking down the River, into the Harbour. It is one Mile from the Water. There is a most beautifull Walk from the House down to the Water. There is a descent, not far from the House. You have a fine Garden—then you descend a few Steps and have another fine Garden—you go down a few more and have another. It is now the dead of Winter, no Verdure, or Bloom to be seen, but in the Spring, Summer, and Fall this Scaene must be very pretty.[9]

*This old mansion, which yet survives, is a graphic
monument of the past time. Its aspect is solemn and
scrupulously aristocratic, and magnificent too, in view of
the means of that day. One may fancy its amplitude and
grave dignity of exterior, with the old lions . . . that stood
rampart on the pillars of the gateway, and there was a fine
terrace overlooking the town. It is but a few years since
these disappeard.*

The Chronicles of Baltimore
by J. Thomas Scharf
1874

᠅᠅᠅ *North, or entrance, front of Mount Clare, circa 1805.* Polychrome decoration, 2¾ inches by 6½ inches, on a settee attributed to John and Hugh Finley of Baltimore (w. 1803-1819). The painting of the house is believed to be by Francis Guy (1760-1820) who was employed by the Finleys from 1804 to 1806. Within the miniature painting, the artist has shown exact details of the house and its dependencies. The lead heraldic beasts purchased by Charles Carroll, Barrister, in 1759 are on the gateposts and lightening rods are indicated on the chimneys tops. *Collection of the Baltimore Museum of Art. Photograph by Duane Suter.*

Garden front of Mount Clare. This elevation of the house is one of the most important examples of English Baroque architecture in Maryland. Mrs. Margaret Carroll had the lunette window in the pediment installed during her alterations to the house in the late 1780's. *Photograph by Duane Suter.*

Staircase seen from the entrance passage. The handrail of the stairs is mahogany, but the balusters were turned from a variety of woods and were originally painted. The door leading to the east hyphen was located in the wall under the stair. The mahogany sideboard, probably Baltimore made, circa 1815, was used by the Carrolls at Mount Clare. Two eighteenth century leather buckets, which held sand and water in case of fire, hang by the stair. *Photograph by Duane Suter.*

⁊⌘ *Margaret Tilghman Carroll (1742-1817)* by Charles Willson Peale (1741-1827), 1770-1771 and 1788. Oil on canvas, 50 inches by 40 inches. One of the pair of portraits of the Barrister and his wife painted after Peale's return from London. Peale's daybook records his working on the portrait from September 1770 to March 1771. Mrs. Carroll is shown with a spray of orange leaves in her right hand. In the background is the garden elevation of Mount Clare. In June 1788, Peale recorded that he altered Mrs. Carroll's portrait. Recent x-rays by the conservation department of the Walters Art Gallery show that the arrangement of the hair was changed and that the oranges on the spray were painted over. The gable of the house was also changed at this time to show the lunette window installed by Mrs. Carroll. *Mount Clare Collection. Photograph by Hughes Company.*

⟨⟩ *Charles Carroll, Barrister, (1723-1783)* by Charles Willson Peale (1741-1827) 1770-1771. Oil on canvas, 49½ inches by 38 inches. This is the companion portrait to Mrs. Carroll's. There is evidence of this painting having been in a fire at some time. The Barrister is shown seated in his study and through the window can be seen a corner of the "Piazza" added in 1768. Beyond is the low brick wall topped with palings enclosing the forecourt. The entrance gates are flanked by wood piers surmounted by lead lions painted to match the piers. *Mount Clare collection.*

Parlor. The panelling is plasterwork, one of the Annapolis regional characteristics of Mount Clare. The door to the right of the fireplace leads to the west hyphen, constructed in 1908. Originally there was a window in this space balancing the one to the left of the fireplace. The mantel was installed by Margaret Tilghman Carroll circa 1788. The set of Louis XV furniture was originally in Mrs. Carroll's wing drawing room. The late eighteenth century, English, painted lire-back chair is a Carroll family piece. The painted fire screen in a mahogany frame at the right of the fireplace belonged to Mrs. Carroll. It is American of the late eighteenth or early nineteenth century. *Photograph by Duane Suter.*

⧈⧈⧈ *Dining room.* The panelling is plasterwork, similar to that in the parlor, entrance passage and stair. The cupboard is one of a pair that flank the fireplace. The mantel is another of those installed by Margaret Tilghman Carroll. All the furniture in this room, except the looking glass, belonged to the Carroll family. The mahogany chairs around the table are part of a set of two arm and six side chairs, American, circa 1785. *Photograph by Duane Suter.*

Carroll bed chamber. The mantel in this room is one of the two remaining in the house from the original building period of 1757-1760. Over the mantel is a copy of John Wesley Jarvis's portrait of Prudence Carnan Gough (1755-1822), Sophie Gough Carroll's mother. Leaning against a bed post is Charles Carroll, Barrister's gold headed malacca walking stick. The American-made Chippendale easy chair belonged to the Carroll family. *Photograph by Duane Suter.*

As with other goods ordered from England, the Barrister was specific in his directions concerning the care of plant material during their shipment. On July 20, 1767 he wrote to William Anderson in London:

> My wife takes much Pleasure in Gardening and sends you a list of Peaches of Each of which she would be Glad if you would send some of the stones of those of them that Can be met with tied up in Different Parcels and the names of Each wrote on the Parcel as Likewise some of the stones of your Best Apricots and Nectarians I would direct in, some of the trees in Boxes but I fear they would be too troublesome However if Montgomerie will Engage to take Care of them and Land them for me at Annapolis I should be Glad if you would send me the Trees mentioned in the List in Boxes whoever you send them by must water them a Little As the Trees will be young and small many of them I suppose may be put in a Box just Enough to Keep them alive During the Passage — I leave it to your Discretion to Judge whether they will be too Troublesome Combersome or Costly or to send me what is Convenient of those mentioned and if you Can meet with anything Curious and will send it us now and then shall be obliged to you.
>
> The Nursery man may Look into Millars Gardeners Dictionary where he will see the names of Each if they are sent I hope the Nursery man will be Carefull that they are Good Thriving young Grafts and well Earthed and of the very same Kind mentioned as they are sometimes Knaves and send Poor worthless Fruit and Different from what is mentioned the Pears should be Grafted on Quince stocks or they will not Last well Here.

Mrs. Carroll's List comprised the following:

2 young Cherrie Trees that have been Buded or Grafted one of the Hertfordshire heart the other the Carnation Cherry

3 Plum Trees that are not more than one years Growth from the Bud or 2 at the most

1 of the Early black Damask Commonly Called the morocco Plum

1 of the violet Predigron Plum

1 of the St Catherine Plum

8 Pear Trees Grafted on Good Free Stocks

1 of the Red Muscadelle, it is also Called the fairest or Supreme

1 of the Skinless or Early Ruselet Pear

1 of the autumn Bergamot

1 of the Iargonelle

1 of the Awarat or Royal Pear

1 of the Dry martin Some times Called the Dry Martin of N Campagne

1 of the Pound Pear, Commonly Called Parkin sous marden or the Black Pear of Worcester —

1 of the Easter St Germain

all these Trees must be put in Boxes of Earth such as are Proper to bring them over Sea the Boxes must be numbered and the names of the Sort that is in Each number be wrote down and sent with other Papers.

Peach Stones of the following Sorts about a Dozen or 2 of each

The Early White Nutmeg

The Early Red Nutmeg

The Bell Cherruse   These part from the Stone

The Early Magdalen

The Bell Grade

The Early Purple

The Old Newington   These adhere to the stone

The Monstrous Pavia of Pompone

The next April, when ordering wines from Scott Pringle Cheap and Co. in Madeira, Carroll added:

> I shall take it as a favour if you^l Please to send me by the Captain who has Promised his Care some of the vines of your best and Largest Eating Grape Black and White not the Cuttings but

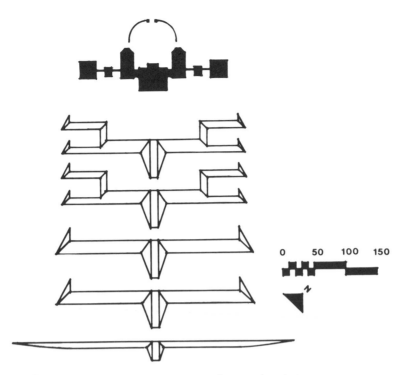

Site plan of Mount Clare, circa 1770, showing the relationship of the house and its connected dependencies to the bowling
green and the falling garden. On line with the door in the center of
the house, leading out from the parlor to the bowling green, grass
ramps connected each level of the flower gardens. The upper two
terraces had smaller terraces at each end at their half levels. To each
side of the falling garden were orchards and vegetable gardens.
Drawing by author.

the vine with the Root to it and put up in a Box with a Little Mold that may Preserve them if
you Could Procure me a Bearing Lemon Tree or two in Boxes with Earth that have been
Inoculated from Good fruit as the Trees Raised from the seed are Generally worthless.

I shall be obliged if you[1] send them to me by the same opportunity or two or three of any
other Trees of Good fruit you may think we Can Manage in this Climate by the help of a Green
House.

The Carrolls sent for garden scythes and watering pots from England and also ordered seeds
for the vegetable gardens including broccoli, cabbage, "Cellery," peas, sorrel, "Colly flower,"
cantaloupe and enough asparagus seed for "3 or 4 beds 30 feet Long and 6 feet Broad." In addition
to Miller's *Gardeners Dictionary*, the Barrister purchased "the Gardeners Callender in one Vol.
Oct° Price five shillings by Doctor Hill."

In the late 1760's another indentured gardener was sent for, along with a tanner, and the
Barrister commented:

if the above servants are Turned of thirty years of age I shall Like them better as they are more
Likely to be Riotous and Troublesome if young. But must take good orderly appearing fellows
tho younger.

Evidently, when the gardener arrived, he was found to be well qualified and knowledgeable.
Several years later, Charles Carroll of Carrollton mentioned in a letter that he had the Barrister's

gardener interview a prospective one before he hired the young man. This was also the same gardener who escorted Mrs. Ambler around the grounds at Mount Clare.

With all the extant information about the vegetable gardens and the orchards (for example the Barrister's letters record that the nursery men, Kennedy and Lee, supplied the fruit trees which were sent from London) it is surprising that there are no surviving records about the flowers, the shrubbery or the ornamental trees planted at Mount Clare. There were no commercial nurseries in Annapolis or Baltimore before the Revolution, so the stock for the flower gardens and other ornamental plantings must have been supplied from private sources.

The Tilghmans' garden at Bay Side could have been one source for seeds and cuttings and plants. Also, the Barrister's sister's garden at Squirrel Neck and her house in Annapolis, and the Carrolls' own garden at their Annapolis house could have been sources. A reference to the way eighteenth century Maryland families obtained plant material is contained in a letter from Charles Carroll of Annapolis to his son in 1770 when that family was enlarging their house and garden on Duke of Gloucester Street: "you may get Honey Locust Pods at Mrs Ogles and Catalpa seeds in y^r owne Garden."

Mrs. William Goldsborough, a cousin of the Barrister and an aunt of his wife, was an avid gardener at her plantation, Peach Blossom, in Talbot County. She received bulbs and seeds and plant material from England including anemones, tulips, peonies, roses, and crocuses. Seeds and cuttings from some of these might well have been sent to Mount Clare. The Carrolls may also have had primroses in their garden. A bookmark made from a piece of paper torn from an eighteenth century Baltimore newspaper still marks the page describing primroses in the Barrister's copy of Miller's *Gardening Dictionary* in the library at Mount Clare.

Starting from the middle of the eighteenth century, there was great interest in Europe and England and America in the science of agriculture and in improving the materials and methods of farming. Along with other major landowners, Charles Carroll was part of this movement, describing himself, in a letter ordering seeds from his agent in England, as one of the "Experiment making Farmers."

Dr. Carroll had begun to shift from planting tobacco to raising wheat and his son continued the change. In the middle of the 1760's, the Barrister wrote to a number of English merchants, in reply to their inquiries about shipping his tobacco on their vessels, that he was not growing any on either his or his wife's plantations. Other business letters indicate that by this time Carroll's primary cash crop was wheat. Most of the Barrister's land under cultivation was used to raise produce to feed the workmen at the Baltimore Company's several furnaces and forges as each of the owners of the company was expected to provide foodstuffs, clothing and tools in proportion to his share of ownership.

The Barrister stressed in his letters that "all the seed I write for may be Fresh and Put in a Dry place in the Ship." In October 1767 he commented that burnet seed sent by Anderson to John Beale Bordley, the foremost agricultural experimenter and pamphleteer in eighteenth century Maryland, was "Either so old or so Damaged in the Ship that it will not Come up" and that "the Loss is a Great Disappointment."

Charles Carroll's orders reflect his interest in improving his wheat and rye, and in experimenting with grasses for his meadows and forage for the large dairy herd he maintained. The herd was probably established in the early 1760's at the time Carroll ordered from Anderson four dozen one gallon pewter milking basins and two dozen large stone butter pots. The Barrister also experimented in raising a flock of sheep.

A letter from the overseer at Mount Clare to the Barrister in Annapolis gives a glimpse of the daily events at Charles Carroll's plantations at the Caves, Carroll's Island and Mount Clare:

Sir

I send the boy Joe down on Saturday Morning with the Veal a pot of Butter and a role of fresher butter, five young pigeons, and some Eggs That was sent from Island. Adam was up the day you went home to Annapolis all were well at the Island but Grace. Adam says the Schooner had then just Returned from Mr. Pressburys with the Cyder and was gitting a load of hay, he has not shelled any of his Corn But says he will get as much as he possible can shelled against the Schooner comes again . . . I have not heard anything from the Caves. I have not any thing very Material to say about this Mount or Plantation as it is not long since you went down, but all are well at present as left us if you have any nails Joe may Bring a few up with him if Price Comes to worke Next Weeke ab^t the Cogg wheel we Must give him a drink of grog once a day and we are Quite out. Please to let me know whether I may get a gallon or two at Balt Town for that Purpose. The day you went away the Painter fell down broke a pane of glass out of one of the Sashes in the house and Split a pot of paint but did not Hurt him self.

I am Sir you Mt Obed^t Hble serv^t
William Heath

Mount Clare April 22, 1769

Charles Carroll had the typical Marylander's passion for horses. In 1764, when the Barrister ordered a watch from London, he wrote:

as I am Concerned in the Blood or Running Breed of Horses I want a Stopt watch with a second Hand to try their speed.

In July 1768 Carroll asked Anderson to:

Look out for an Arabian Horse for me But on Consideration I shall like a Barb better as they are more Likely to Retain their Spirit when old are better to Breed Riding Horses from and Besides come Cheaper so that I would have you Git me one of that Breed and kind of a True one Spirited and Shapely to be Got for the Price Limited in my Letter above mentioned that is not Exceeding one hundred Guineas.

The reputation colonial Marylanders enjoyed for hospitality on their plantations and at their houses in Annapolis was well deserved. When Daniel Dulany the Elder, a close friend of both Dr. Carroll and the Barrister, died in 1753, the inventory of his personal property included 166 gallons of various wines. The brick-vaulted portion of the basement at Mount Clare may have served as the Barrister's wine cellar. In addition, he must also have maintained a wine cellar at his house in Annapolis. On December 6, 1766 Charles Carroll began a correspondence with the merchant firm Scott Pringle and Company on the island of Madeira, saying:

Gent

I had the Pleasure of Mr Murrays Company as he went through this Province and by his Recommendation I Desire you will by the first Vessell Coming to Annapolis send me a Pipe of the Best Madeira wine as it is for my own Table use I would have it of the very Prime Kind for the Cost of which you will be pleased to Draw on Mr William Anderson Merchant in London and send with your Bill the Inclosed Letter I would if you Can have the wine two or three years old or more if it Can be Got of Equal Goodness in Quality with what may be Bought of the Last vintages and Tho' it should Cost me more I shall willingly allow it. . . .

Mr Murray Promised me he would mention me Particularly to you and as I shall annually write for a Pipe I hope I shall have no Reason to Change my Correspondence. If at any time a pipe of Superfine old or new is to be met with and you will Lay it by and write me word I will send orders to Mr Anderson to pay your Draft for it and my Directions to you to Ship it to me.

I am Gent y^r M h^{ble} Servt

Cha. Carroll

On December 7 the following year, the Barrister wrote to the same firm, now Scott Pringle Cheap & Co.:

> I have . . . Rec^d safe by the sloop *Potts* the Pipe of Madeira sent by Her to me the Flavor of it I Like very well shall be a Better Judge of it two or three years Hence & Have Laid it by for about that Time Be Pleased to send me in by Capt Read a Pipe of the same Prime Kind for my own use . . . Shall be obliged if in y^r next you will Let me Know whereabouts the Best Malmsey Comes p^r H^hd or p^r Cask & whether a Little of it will not mix well with & Improve the Madeira Table wine & about what Quantity to the Pipe

In later letters he asked that the maderia sent him be "of the Prime full kind and the oldest you can Get" and that the Malmsey be "of the best and the Richest."

Through his usual agent in London the Barrister ordered port, "best Rhenish," Battavia Anock, "opporto Southhampton" and French Brandy. He complained to Anderson in the fall of 1766,

> I have often Desired the Captain to Pick me up some Good French Brandy in the Downs as they may do it Cheap and they have Promised but failed so must have it with the Duties on.[7]

Charles Carroll's letters show not only his enjoyment of life, including the pleasures of the table, they also record his losing battle against his increasing girth. In the summer of 1758 his invoice to Anderson in London included a new suit which Carroll wrote to be "fassionable," but "not made in the Extremity of the Fashion" and in the accompanying letter requested that:

> The Cloaths I would have made by Jonathan Reynolds a Taylor in New Court Carey street Lincolns Inn fields who has my measure but I believe I am through Laziness something Fatter than when I left you but in Case he should have Lost my measure Inclosed I send it Taken here.

Ten years later, the battle lost, he asked Anderson to send "A Pair of Exercising Leads."

In the 1760's the Barrister and his wife were among the few families, along with the Ogles, the Dulanys, and Charles Carroll of Annapolis, who maintained town residences in Annapolis in addition to their country houses. The decade preceding the Revolution was Annapolis's Golden Age, and its winter season—when the legislature was in session, the Assembly Rooms and the theatre were open and the Maryland Jockey Club's race meetings were held—was one of the most brilliant in the American colonies.

William Eddis described the city shortly after his arrival in 1769:

> Several of the most opulent families have here established their residence; and hospitality is the characteristic of the inhabitants.

and

> I am persuaded there is not a town in England of the same size as Annapolis which can boast a greater number of fashionable and handsome women.

Later, after the Rev. Jonathan Boucher had returned to London because of his Loyalist sympathies, he remembered Annapolis in the early 1770's:

> It was the genteelest town in North America, and many of its inhabitants were highly respectable, as to station, fortune, and education. I hardly know a town in England so desirable to live in as Annapolis then was. It was the seat of Government, and the residence of the Governor, and all the great officers of state, as well as the most eminent lawyers, physicians, and families of opulence and note.

☙ *My Lady's Visit* by Francis B. Mayer (1827-1899), circa 1876. oil on canvas, 31 ½ by 46 inches.
Mayer used the porch on Charles Carroll, Barrister's Annapolis house for this painting, and depicted
the view of Annapolis harbor from the Carrolls' lawn. The sedan chair is based upon the one believed to
have been used by Governor and Mrs. Robert Eden in Annapolis from 1769 to 1766. *From the collection
of the Maryland Historical Society, on deposit from the Peabody Institute.*

Charles Carroll's Annapolis house sat on almost four acres, overlooking both the harbor and
the mouth of the Severn River. It fronted on Green Street, and its grounds ran down to the Severn
where the Barrister's warehouse and dock and those of his brother-in-law were located. The
house, in which four generations of Carrolls lived, is no longer standing. Rebuilt in the early
nineteenth century after the family had sold the property, the house was demolished early in this
century. According to the Federal Tax of 1798, it was a frame house 40 feet wide by 32 feet deep
with a detached brick kitchen, a brick stable and a smoke house. It is believed to have been gambrel
roofed and, in silhouette, it must have been similar to the Jonas Green house on Charles Street in
Annapolis.

In spite of its relatively small size, the Barrister's house was considered of the most opulent
in the city. Its rooms were probably paneled, possibly with plaster paneling similar to that at
Mount Clare. The 1798 Federal Direct Tax valued the house, its dependencies and its surrounding
two acres at $1,650.00. This was more than the values of the larger, newer and very elegant Scott,
Ridout or Ogle houses.

The most distinctive feature of the Carrolls' house was the porch on its garden elevation. The
house originally had a pair of parlors across its garden side, each with two windows overlooking
the garden and the water. When the porch was added, one window in the east parlor, by then used
as a dining room, became a door leading onto the porch. The construction of the porch probably
dates from the time of the Barrister's marriage. In September 1763, his invoice to William
Anderson includes nails and brass door hardware sufficient for minor alterations to a house. Since
Mount Clare was recently completed, this material was likely for the Annapolis house.

The wood porch was eight feet deep and almost eleven feet wide. Across the front was a tall arched opening, set within pilasters, and a low arch was on each side. Along each side was a bench, and from the center of the front of the porch a wide flight of steps led down to the lawn.

Francis Meyer, whose sketches of Annapolis in the middle of the nineteenth century are some of our best records of the early architecture of that city, made a series of drawings of the Barrister's porch. They show its details as well as views of the market place and harbor and the distant Chesapeake Bay as seen from the porch. These sketches were later used as the basis of his painting, *My Lady's Visit.*

Porches were uncommon in America before the Revolution, but a number of Annapolis houses had architecturally sophisticated porches of a size large enough to be used for sitting. The Scott and Ridout houses have porches, both with Roman Doric detailing. Governor Eden's house had two somewhat smaller ones, and Charles Carroll of Carrollton built the largest of the pre-Revolutionary porches as part of his additions to his father's house. These elegant porches, most of which looked over the terraced gardens of their houses and out across the Chesapeake Bay to the distant Eastern Shore, are evocative of the leisurely, polished life of the Annapolis aristocracy in the decade preceding the American Revolution.[10]

In the same invoice of September 1763, in which he sent for door hardware, the Barrister ordered: "3 Glass stands of Different Sizes for the Middle of a Table and Glasses for Syllabubs Sweet Meats, etc. Sufficient" for the dining room of his Annapolis house. Three years later the Carrolls ordered the following for their bed chamber in their town house:

1 Good English Carpet wth Lively Colours 12/4 by 14

1 neat four Post Mahogany Bedstead 6 feet 4 Inches Long and 4 foot 6 Inches wide and 6 foot 11 Inches in hight from the Floor to the Tester Frame

1 Suit of Curtains and valins for Ditto of a Good Furniture Cotton of a Large Pattern and Rich Colours to be well Fitted and to Hang upon brads or with Hooks and Eyes so as to be Easily taken up or Down

2 pair of window Curtains 2 yards and 3 inches Long

2 Single Ditto one yard and 3/4 Long

2 Spare yards Cotton and 2 Dozen of the Binding

1 Neat Quilt for the Bed —

1 fine Cotton Counter Pain 9/4 and a half —

10 pieces best Genteel paper for a bed Chamber

2 pieces of Bordering for Ditto to suit the Furniture before mentioned but not too Dark

1 Good Mahogany Beaureau wrought Furniture

1 Good Mahogany Dressing Glass wth Drawers at the Bottom —

The same invoice also includes another order for wallpaper: "7 pieces Common paper for a Bed Chamber with a Light stone Colour Ground and blue or Purple Figures," as well as "I piece Matting for Passages."

Charles Carroll's library of law books was kept in the house on Green Street, and it was there that he used a richly carved Maryland-made chest-on-chest containing a fitted desk behind a drawer. The green silk curtains which the Carrolls ordered through their London agent were for the parlor and dining room of this house. There had been similar curtains in these rooms since Dr. Carroll first sent to England for them in 1744.

To get around Annapolis, the Barrister had ordered in the summer of 1760:

one four Wheeled post Chariot made Light and Fashionable without a Box strong and neat with Plain simple strong springs Lined with Green Cloth Painted and ornamented Fashionably with the Inclosed Coat of Arms with saddle and strong Good Harness for a pair of Horses and Crest in Brass Plates on the Harness and a spare set of Glasses that may be Provided against Accidents suppose may be Got Compleat for about seventy or eighty pounds would not have it of the small Dapper Fashion but of the Roomy sort as it is not for Travelling into the Country with but for Town use and they answer much better than heavy Chariots with Boxes as our Horses are but small and Ground Deep and sandy.

In a letter accompanying the invoice he sent more directions for the coach, including: "I would have if Can be fixed Convinently a stand behind and a Couple of straps for a servant." After his marriage, Charles Carroll sent for harness for four horses with postillion riders,[11] indicating that he and his wife used the coach for longer trips, perhaps as far as the the 26 mile journey up to Mount Clare.

In the spring of 1771 the Barrister and his wife planned to sail for England. Charles Carroll hoped that the waters at the spas might cure him of what he referred to as "my Troublesome annual vistant the fever and Ague" and the trip would be his wife's first opportunity to see London and the country which colonial Americans always referred to as "home."

The former governor, Horatio Sharpe, living in retirement at Whitehall, his plantation across the river from Annapolis, wrote to his brother, Philip Sharpe, on May 27:

> You will probably in the Course of the Summer meet at Bath or Tunbridge a Mr. Carroll of this Provience who with his Wife went to England about three Weeks ago in hopes of receiving some Benefit from those Waters."

Charles Carroll of Carrollton gave the Barrister a letter of introduction to Edmund Jennings, a former Marylander whose family had returned to England in the 1750's, saying:

> Dr Sir:
>
> This will be delivered to you by Mr Carroll, with whose company you will be much pleased. His lady is a very amiable woman, tho' somewhat reserved to strangers. However, on a better acquaintance that reserve will entirely wear off, and then the goodness of her heart will charm you.

The Carrolls were away from Maryland for 18 months. While they were in London they attended several court functions including Queen Charlotte's birthday ball. The Barrister's letters from England are now lost, but Charles Carroll of Carrollton's reply to one sheds light on Margaret Carroll's opinion of life in London. On December 2, 1771 Carrollton wrote to the Barrister: "I was not surprised to hear she prefers ye domestic amusements of Maryland to ye vanities of St. James. The society of a few choice friends is worth all ye pomp & emptyness of a court." Finally, the Carrolls sailed for home, and on Thursday, September 17, 1772 the *Maryland Gazette* announced: "This Morning arrived here on the *Nelly* Frigate, Capt. *Archibald Greig*, from *London*, in whom came Passengers *Charles Carroll*, Esq; of this City, Barrister, and his Lady."

After the Carrolls' return, their orders for goods from London were sent to a new firm, Wallace, Davidson and Johnson. The business affairs of their long time agent, William Anderson, had become so hopelessly entangled that finally trustees had to be appointed to settle his debts. The letters from Joshua Johnson in London to the Barrister indicate how anxious the recently established firm was for Charles Carroll's business. They traced down a wine cooler which the Barister had sent to Anderson to be repaired and shipped it back, but a tea board sent for repairs at the same time as the cooler, was never found.[12]

As the 1770's progressed, the storm clouds of the Revolution grew darker and darker. Although the Barrister had not taken part in the proprietary government since 1761, when he last

Chest-on-chest with a fitted desk behind the drawer in the lower section. Mahogany, height 99 inches, width 48 inches. Made in Maryland and used by Charles Carroll, Barrister, in his Annapolis house. The carved mouldings on this chest-on-chest are similiar in design and quality to carved mouldings found in Annapolis houses of the same period. *Photograph courtesy of Benjamin Ginsburg Antiquary.*

served in the Lower House of the Assembly, he was closely in touch with leaders of both houses of the legislature. The interconnected economic and social ties among Maryland's landed and merchant families, as well as the Carrolls' wide family connections, kept Charles Carroll aware of and part of the political arguments and discussions. His father-in-law, Matthew Tilghman, was one of Talbot County's representatives in the Lower House from 1768 until 1774 and he served as its Speaker in 1773 and 1774. Numerous cousins also took active roles in the legislature in the years immediately preceding the war.

After the Maryland Assembly adjourned in April 1774, a convention of representatives of the counties was formed and met first on June 22 the same year. Charles Carroll, Barrister, was one of Anne Arundel County's delegates. From that time on, he played an active role in the events leading up to final break with England. In the General Assembly of 1777, the first called under the new State of Maryland, the Barrister served as a senator and continued in that capacity throughout the war years.

During the Revolution, the Carrolls spent as much time at Mount Clare as possible, and it probably was during this period that the house was used as a year-round residence for the first time. With the collapse of the Colonial government, there was no social life in Annapolis as Charles and Margaret Carroll had known it. The fall races of the Jockey Club were cancelled in 1775. In June 1776 Robert Eden, the last British governor remaining in the colonies, sailed from Annapolis. Friends of the Carrolls whose sympathies were with the Crown had already either fled to England or were living as unobtrusively as possible on their country plantations.[13] In February 1776 Mrs. Benjamin Ogle wrote from the family's house in Annapolis to her mother-in-law, who was caught in England by the hostilities: "Annapolis is vastly dull many Families having left it and almost every one preparing to go—we have had neither Balls or Routs and very little Dining & Supping out. The same dull Scene forever." As the war progressed, troops of the Continental Army were quartered in Annapolis, and the harbor was filled with ships of the new navy. There was little in the merchants' stores, and provisions in the market were not as plentiful as before. All of this made living at Mount Clare preferable to Annapolis, except when governmental duties required that the Barrister be in the capital.

Another reason the Carrolls would have preferred the quiet country life at Mount Clare over the noise and crowded conditions in wartime Annapolis was that they at last had a family. Two children were born to the Barrister and his wife in the late 1770's. After 16 years of marriage— Charles Carroll was 56, his wife 37 — they must have given up hope of having children. A daughter, Margaret Clare, was born on June 22, 1779, probably at Mount Clare, and baptized at St. Paul's Church in Baltimore on December sixth. There is no record of the birth or name or baptism of the second child, but, according to family tradition, the two were twins. The Carrolls' children were not strong and did not survive infancy. In spite of the care and attention they must have received one child died before April 1780 and Margaret Clare died at Mount Clare in January 1781.[14]

The Barrister had inherited a sizable fortune from his father which he had increased in the years preceding the Revolution. In spite of the difficult economic conditions during the war, the Carroll estate was still one of the largest in Maryland. Now, without direct heirs, it was important that provision be made to pass the fortune on within the family.

On August seventh, seven months after his daughter's death, Charles Carroll drew up his will. His niece, Mrs. Mary Maccubbin Brice, was to receive £2,000. Susanna Maccubbin, another niece, and a nephew, Charles Maccubbin, would each receive £500. Francis Fairbrother, who had been his clerk for 25 years, would receive the warehouse and dock in Annapolis for life. His widow, Margaret Tilghman Carroll, would receive the use of either the house in Annapolis or

Mount Clare for life, as well as one-half of the income of the estate. Nicholas Maccubbin, the Barrister's eldest nephew, was named the residuary legatee provided he took the surname Carroll.

In March 1783 the Barrister, already suffering from one of his recurring fevers, caught a severe cold and, after a brief illness, died at Mount Clare on March 23rd. On the day of his death, he added a codicil to his will. His widow was to have Mount Clare for life, after which it would pass to James Maccubbin, the fourth of his sister's five sons. James also would have to take the name Carroll in order to inherit Mount Clare.

In June of that summer, John Ridout, the Carrolls' neighbor in Annapolis, wrote to the former governor, Horatio Sharpe, in England giving him news about their friends and described the Barrister's death:

> In Consequence of Baltimore Towns flourishing so much an offer was made Bar^r Carroll last winter by some Gent there to pay him for ever an annual Rent of £600 sty for 60 acres of his Land at the Mount to be laid out in Lotts on the water below his House towards Patapsco Ferry, he accepted the offer & the Survayer proceeded to lay off the Land, it was unluckely a very Cold Day yet the Bar^r feverish as he was would quit his Fire Side & be down with the Survayor, a violent Cold was the Consequence of his Imprudence which brought on a Fever that in a short time carried him to his grave, . . . He had he told me when I was last at his House been paid off under the Debt Act three fourths of the Debts due him but he left a very fine Estate. One half to Mrs. Carroll and the rest among some of his Nephews, the children of Mr. Nicholas MaCubbin, the eldest of whom is the principal Legatee & who in consequence of the will takes the Name of Carroll.[15]

Charles Carroll, Barrister, died at the close of the Revolutionary period when conditions were still unsettled, and no record has survived of his burial. It has been stated, however, that he was interred in the Carroll vault in St. Anne's churchyard in Annapolis where his father and brother, and later his wife, were buried.

His obituary appeared in the Friday, March twenty-eighth, issue of *The Maryland Journal and Baltimore Advertiser:*

> On Sunday Evening last, departed this Life, at Mount Clare, the Honourable CHARLES CARROLL, Esq., Barrister at Law in the 59th Year of his Age. — He was distinguished, through Life, as a zealous and firm Advocate for the Rights and Liberties of his Country, and many Years, before the Revolution, enjoyed the Confidence of his Fellow-Citizens, as their Representative in the Legislature; but declining that Trust from bodily infirmities, he led the Life of a private Citizen nobly declining the Acceptance of proffered *proprietary Distinctions,* till the Oppressions of America roused her virtuous Sons to vindicate her injured Rights; — He was among the first Citizens of this State who, associated for the Purpose, and sacrificing every domestic Ease and Convenience, that Wealth could afford, he discharged the important duties of a Member of the Convention and Council of Safety of this State, to the great injury of his Health. — He was one of the principal Framers of our Constitution and Bill of Rights, and, on their Establishments, was elected by the Voice of his Countrymen, a Senator, in which respectable and dignified Station, he has served with great Reputation for Six Years past. — He was remarkable for his Hospitality and Politeness, particularly to Strangers — his natural Sweetness of Manners, polished by Travel and a liberal Education, endeared him to his Friends; — he was an affectionate Husband, and an indulgent Master; and the Fortitude exhibited in his last Moments, of which he was perfectly sensible, evinces that he left this Life and all its Enjoyments, with perfect Resignation to the Divine Will, and certain Hopes of Happiness hereafter. In this Gentleman, the Public has lost a faithful and able Servant, a Wife an indulgent Husband, and his Acquaintance, a sincere and valuable Friend.

CAPE HENRY

Curratuck Inlet

Roanoke Inlet

A MAP of
the moſt INHABITED part of
VIRGINIA
containing the whole PROVINCE of
MARYLAND
with Part of
PENSILVANIA, NEW JERSEY and NORTH CAROLINA
Drawn by
Joshua Fry & Peter Jefferson
in 1775.

To the Right Honourable, George Dunk Earl of Halifax First Lord Commiſſioner,
and to the Reſt of the Right Honourable and Honourable Commiſſioners, for TRADE and PLANTATIONS.
This Map is moſt humbly Inſcribed to their Lordſhips,
By their Lordſhips
Most Obedient & most devoted humble Servt. Thos. Jefferys.

1   2

⟨⟨ Cartouche illustrating a warehouse and dock from Fry and Jefferson's map of Virginia and Maryland, 1751. Engraving on paper, 8 by 10 inches. Charles Carroll had a warehouse and dock at the foot on his property in Annapolis. At Mount Clare he used either the Baltimore Iron Work's dock at the mouth of Gwynn's Falls or the dock at his shipyard on Carroll's Point. *Collection of Mr. and Mrs. Thomas G. Young III, Photograph by Duane Suter.*

IV

THE BARRISTER'S CAREER

W hen Charles Carroll, Barrister, was studying at the Middle Temple, he thought of remaining in England, but his father discouraged the idea, advising him instead to "fix your Eye for future Life in Maryland."

Carroll returned to Annapolis in the summer of 1755, and for the next several months he was preoccupied with his father's final illness. After Dr. Carroll's death in September, the Barrister was able to turn his attention to the family's business enterprises and to his own career.

In October 1755 he was admitted to practice before the Provincial Court of Maryland. In November, he was admitted to the Anne Arundel County Court and by the following February the Barrister was practicing before the Court of Chancery.

Because his legal papers have not survived, it has sometimes been assumed that Carroll did not have an active law practice, but his high reputation during his lifetime and his extensive law library indicate that he did pursue a legal career.

The only known record of a fee paid to Charles Carroll is found in Samuel Chase's accounts of the costs of his unfinished house in Annapolis before he sold it to Edward Lloyd in 1771. For legal services on behalf of Chase, the Barrister's fee was £6.15.10.

In July 1773 Charles Carroll of Carrollton, in writing to his father, referred to an unspecified legal case involving their cousin, Anthony Carroll. Anthony Carroll was represented by a lawyer named Ashton; the Barrister represented the other party.

The Barrister attended the various courts before which he pleaded cases. These sessions were social occasions as well as business ones, giving friends and members of families living far apart on their plantations opportunities to visit one another. When the courts were held outside of Annapolis, Margaret Carroll sometimes accompanied her husband. In the fall of 1765 Carroll wrote to William Anderson: "We have Just had a Glimpse of our Cousin Jemmy while over at the Provincial Court."

Dr. Carroll was representing Anne Arundel County in the Lower House of the Proprietary Assembly at the time of his death, and in March 1756 the Barrister was elected to complete his father's term. He was re-elected to the two following Assemblies and served until the later one was adjourned in May 1761.

Carroll, as his father had been before him, was a member of the country party and in opposition to the court party, composed of supporters of the Calvert family which owned Maryland. After 1761 the Barrister's only official connection with the government of the province was as a member of the building committee for the new "Stadt House," to which he was appointed in 1769.

Before and during the American Revolution, Charles Carroll was among the respected leaders who helped make the transition from the established proprietary government to the new state government more orderly than it was in some of the other colonies. John Ridout referred to the Barrister's actions during this period as "very moderate & honorable."[1]

The Barrister represented Anne Arundel County in a convention that met in Annapolis from June 22 to 25, 1774. The convention was called to determine Maryland's response to the Boston Port Bill, by which the British parliament had closed the port of Boston in retaliation for the Boston Tea Party. The Proprietary Assembly had adjourned in April, and this convention, in effect, was the beginning of a provisional government. A total of eight conventions were called through July 1776, in all of which the Barrister served. His father-in-law, Matthew Tilghman, chaired all but the seventh of these conventions which acted as the de facto government.[2]

By the time of the fifth convention in July 1775, the delegates realized that an executive branch of their extra-legal government was necessary. They formed a Council of Safety for that purpose, and both Charles Carroll and Matthew Tilghman were members. The Barrister was also appointed to a committee "to consider of the ways and means to put this Province into the best state of defence."

Robert Eden, the last British governor in the thirteen colonies, still resided in his house in Annapolis, and his authority as governor was still acknowledged. In January 1776 Charles Carroll invited Governor Eden to a dinner party at his house on Green Street to which he also asked his father-in-law and several other members of the Council of Safety, which was then in session. In addition, Carroll invited those the Governor described as the "most distinguished members of the Whig party": Thomas Johnson who, the following year, would become the first governor of the State of Maryland; Samuel Chase and Thomas Stone, both of whom would sign the Declaration of Independence in six months' time; and James Holliday, one of the most prominent lawyers in Maryland. The object of the dinner was to give them an opportunity to discuss, privately and quietly, ways by which they could "disperse the cloud that has almost overshadowed and is ready to bust upon us."

By summer, it was obvious that Eden had to depart, and on June 23, 1776 the *HMS Fowey*, under a flag of truce, arrived in the Annapolis harbor to take the governor aboard. The entire Council of Safety, including Charles Carroll, Barrister, escorted Eden to his barge where they took "an affectionate leave" of the governor.

From the porch of the Carrolls' house, the family could have seen the *Fowey* leave the harbor and sail down the Chesapeake Bay. As the ship passed out of view, six generations of proprietary family government came to an end. Eleven days later, on July third, the provisional government adopted Maryland's declaration of independence which Charles Carroll was credited with writing.

The Barrister was elected to the ninth convention which opened that August. Its major business was to be the important task of framing a constitution for Maryland. Carroll, however, resigned almost immediately, along with Samuel Chase and Rezin Hammond, because he believed that the opinions of the Anne Arundel County voters regarding a new state government were "incompatible with good government and the public peace and happiness." Although not a part of the convention, Carroll was appointed to the committee which drafted Maryland's first constitution and is believed to have exerted the major influence upon its provisions.

This same year, he was appointed a judge of the General Court of Maryland but declined because of his poor health.

On February 5, 1777 the first General Assembly of the State of Maryland met, and the Barrister, who had been elected a member of the Senate, attended. His father-in-law and several cousins also served in the Senate. Other cousins were elected to the House of Delegates. Charles Carroll continued to serve in the state Senate and was a member at the time of his death in March 1783.

After the Barrister's death neither an inventory was made of his personal property, nor were administrative accounts kept of the value of his estate. Only through letters, land records and the few surviving business papers can Charles Carroll's wide-ranging financial affairs be understood.

The income which supported the Carrolls and made Mount Clare possible did not come from tobacco, the major crop in the Chesapeake region. As early as the 1740's, Dr. Carroll had realized that the "sot weed" upon which the planters of Maryland and Virginia were so dependent was too susceptible to the vagaries of the weather and overseas market conditions. Indeed, he realized that being only a planter would never provide the estate he hoped to leave to his children. The fortune which the doctor began accumulating shortly after his arrival in Annapolis and which his son, the Barrister, increased was based upon mercantile, financial and industrial activities.

At his plantations on Carroll's Island and at the Caves, the Barrister grew foodstuffs to supply his share for the Baltimore Company's workmen. In addition, on these plantations and at Mount Clare he planted wheat which he ground at his two mills along the east bank of Gwynns Falls. The extent of Carroll's milling activities is illustrated in a letter to Thomas Ringgold at Chestertwon, dated February 25, 1761:

> Sir:
>
> The flower I was making Ready when you was in Baltimore has Been Brought to Town and part of it Disposed of before I Received your Letter. But I have sixty seven Barrels now here which I have Acquainted M[r] Joseph Galloway with and Desired Him to send for it and I will have Eighty or one hundred Barrels more Ready for you in a month from this Date. Could get it sooner but am obliged to Finish some work for a Customer whose wheat is now at my Mill . . . I do not know what to do with Pennsylvania Currency but will take Gold or silver or if it be more Convenient to you will take a Bill at the sailing of the Ships at sixty per Cent Exchange
>
> I am sir you most H[ble] servt
> C. C.

Several years later, Charles Carroll of Carrollton wrote to his father that he had run out of flour at his house in Annapolis and had been "obliged to purchase a barell of the barrister." In addition, the Barrister owned a bakery in Annapolis which he supplied with flour from his mills.

Dr. Carroll had established a boatyard on Carroll's Point on the Patapsco River. At the time of the doctor's death his son complained that "Ship building is not to be carried on here but at a great Expense and Risque." However, the Barrister continued the family's ship building operation and in March 1776 wrote, "We got the ship *Defence* into the river this morning."

At the foot of his garden in Annapolis, where Compromise Steet now runs, Carroll had a dock and a warehouse. Advertisements in the *Maryland Gazette* in 1757 show that he had salt, sugar, furniture and bar-iron for sale at his warehouse. In 1781, during the war when there was little or no mercantile activity, the Barrister rented the warehouse to Adam Rebb, a cooper.

The Barrister inherited eleven lots in Annapolis from his father.[3] Later, he also owned lots in London Town and Elk Ridge and had a house and lot in Baltimore Town, which he leased. When Carroll sold the Baltimore property in 1766 for 100 pounds sterling, he agreed to take "Pensylvania money or Pieces of Eight" if the purchaser, John Scerce, wished.

Charles Carroll's major land holdings were in Western Maryland. His father had taken out patents on almost 28,500 acres and had purchased 3,000 more. By the time of his death, the doctor had sold all but 8,700 acres. Dr. Carroll usually surpassed his anticipated profit of 400 percent on his land ventures. The Barrister continued his father's interest in Frederick County land. He acquired more tracts, eventually holding over 15,400 acres in that county. After the middle of the eighteenth century this was the most rapidly developing part of Maryland, and by the time of Carroll's death he had sold 7,000 acres, mostly in parcels of less than 200 acres, to settlers as they established farms. In addition to the land still held for development in Frederick County, and his three plantations which totaled 4,500 acres, the Barrister left over 3,000 acres in Anne Arundel, Baltimore and possibly Prince George's counties.

Like other very well-to-do men, Charles Carroll let money out at interest. There were no banks in Maryland until after the Revolution, and the Barrister, Charles Carroll of Annapolis, and others like them were the only sources for borrowing funds. In 1759, the Barrister listed the debts owed to him which totaled £654.7.11 sterling and £5,621.2.10 in Maryland currency. The list of those who had borrowed from him was wide-ranging and included two of his overseers, Patrick Graham and Philip Dougherty; John Smith, Sr., a shipwright at the boatyard on the Patapsco; Dr. John Stevenson in Baltimore Town and Dr. George Steuart in Annapolis; and Charles Wallace, one of the Annapolis merchants who later founded Wallace, Davison and Johnson. The list also included such well-known people as Charles Ridgely, Col. Charles Hammond, Benjamin Tasker and Edward Lloyd III.

The best known of the Barrister's investments was his one-fifth interest in the Baltimore Company. His father had been one of its founders in 1731 and had acted as the managing partner. The enterprise was successful from the start, and by 1734 the company had 81 workmen. At the time of the Revolution, the Barrister's interest was valued at £14,000.

The Baltimore Company primarily produced bar and pig iron. Each partner received iron in proportion to his interest in the firm which he shipped to England to sell as advantageously as possible. In the early 1770's the partners were exporting approximately 3,100 tons of bar and pig iron annually.

The Baltimore Company operated a forge and a furnace on its lands west of Mount Clare. The Company also had a dock on this property, at the mouth of Gwynns Falls. It had two other forges. One, the Mount Royal Forge, was located one-and-a-half miles north of Baltimore Town along Jones Falls, and the other, the Hockley Forge, was on the west branch of the Patapsco River near Elk Ridge.

The Company owned over 30,000 acres. Some of this land held iron ore, but most of it was forested and was needed to supply the large quantities of wood necessary for making charcoal. In addition to free and indentured workers, the Baltimore Company owned 155 slaves valued at £6,200.

It is impossible to estimate the size of the income the Barrister realized from his varied sources, but one can understand that he could well afford to live a life which the historian W. Stoll Holt, in summing up the Barrister's career, described as that of "a sensible, cultured patrician."

North entrance doors with rusticated surround. *Drawing by author.*

South, or garden, front of Mount Clare. The wall is laid in all-header bond, a characteristic of the Annapolis region. The centers of the four pilasters are glazed headers. The bricks in the flat arches over the window and door openings are rubbed and gauged. The lunette window in the pediment dates from the late 1780's when it replaced the original circular window. The window sashes are twentieth century replacements in nineteenth century frames (except for the frame of the lunette window which dates from the 1780's). *H.A.B.S.*

V

MARGARET TILGHMAN CARROLL: 1783-1817

W hen General Cornwallis's troops marched out to surrender at Yorktown on October 19, 1781, their band played *The World Turned Upside Down*. The music was prophetic, because the world which began that day for Britain's former colonies was quite different from that which had ended on July 4, 1776.

In the spring of 1783 the world for Charles Carroll's widow was also turned upside down, and a new life began. Margaret Tilghman Carroll's husband and children had died. By the terms of her husband's will she had only a life interest in Mount Clare and its contents. In addition to the income from her own money, she would receive half of the income from the Barrister's estate. John Ridout had remarked in his letter to Horatio Sharpe that Charles Carroll's estate, although diminished, was still sizable. Mrs. Carroll could afford to continue living at Mount Clare on the same scale as she and her husband had before the Revolution.

The former political, economic and social world of Annapolis, of which the Carrolls were a part, had been swept away by the Revolution. Neighbors and friends—the Dulanys, the Taskers, former Governor Sharpe, the Edens — were gone. By 1783 brash, bustling, fast-growing Baltimore had emerged as the commercial and social capital of the Chesapeake region. Buildings in the new Federal style were being erected there. The best craftsmen and silversmiths and furniture makers were now established in Baltimore. When Dr. Carroll had begun the first house on his Georgia patent, Baltimore was two miles away and had a population of about 500; now with a population of 8,000 the town was growing closer to Mount Clare.[1]

Mrs. Carroll's early widowhood must have been comforted by having her sister living nearby in Baltimore. Anna Maria Tilghman married her first cousin, Colonel Tench Tilghman, in June 1783, their wedding having been delayed due to the Barrister's death the previous March. Tench Tilghman had been one of General Washington's aides-de-camp and his military secretary. As a mark of the esteem in which the Commander-in-Chief held the colonel, Tilghman was selected by Washington to carry the news of Cornwallis's surrender at Yorktown to Congress. Now, with the war ended, Tench Tilghman settled in Baltimore where he opened a mercantile business in partnership with Robert Morris, the Philadelphia financier.

On May 19, 1784 Margaret Carroll made a number of purchases from her brother-in-law including five cotton "Petty Coats" and twelve yards of black gauze. Although still in mourning, she also bought a box of artificial flowers and a stylish pierced-bone dressing case. Mrs. Carroll evidently changed some of the curtains and chair covers at Mount Clare, for at the same time she purchased 72 yards of striped muslin and 49 yards of shalloon.

In August 1784 Tench Tilghman received a letter from General Washington inquiring about the construction of the orangery at Mount Clare. The Barrister and Mrs. Carroll had known the Washingtons in the years before the Revolution when the Washingtons regularly came up to

Plan of orangery. At the right side of the orangery were steps leading down to a "furnace" or fireplace which heated underfloor hot air ducts. Archaeological investigation has located the ducts which were sketched by Tench Tilghman in his letter to George Washington of August 18, 1784. The ducts leading to the center chimney are shown by dashed lines. The north half of the building, believed to have been used as work areas or living quarters by the gardener, has yet to be excavated. *Drawing by author.*

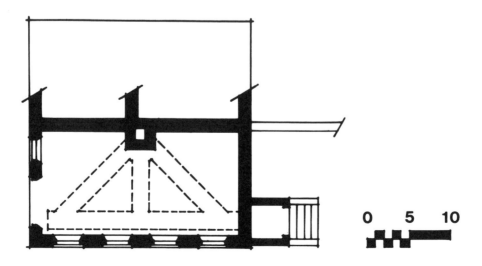

Annapolis for the social life during the racing season. Mrs. Carroll had probably seen them again in Annapolis in December 1783 when the General resigned his commission before Congress, which was meeting there in the State House. The following March Washington wrote in closing, in a letter to Tilghman, "My best respects, in which Mrs. Washington joins, are presented to Mrs. Tilghman and Mrs. Carroll." The gardens at Mount Clare were among the finest in the Chesapeake region in the eighteenth century, and Washington was obviously acquainted with their general design because he now wrote:

Mount Vernon, August 11, 1784.

Dear Sir: I shall essay the finishing of my green house this fall, but find that neither myself, nor any person about me is so well skilled in the internal construction as to proceed without a probability at least of running into errors.

Shall I for this reason, ask the favor of you to give me a short description of the Green-House at Mrs. Carrolls? I am persuaded, now that I planned mine upon too contracted a scale. My house is (of Brick) 40 feet by 24, in the outer dimensions, and half the width disposed of for two rooms, back of the part designed for the green house; leaving the latter in the clear not more than about 37 by 10. As there is no cover on the walls yet, I can raise them to any height, the information I wish to obtain is,

The dimensions of Mrs. Carroll's Green-house. what kind of floor is to it. how high from that floor to the bottom of the window frame, what height the windows are bottom to top, how high from the top to the ceiling of the house, whether the ceiling is flat, or of what kind. whether the heat is conveyed by flues, and a grate. whether those flues run all around the House, the size of them without, and in the clear. Whether they join the wall, or are separate and distinct from it, if the latter, how far they are apart, with any other suggestions you may conceive necessary.

I should be glad to hear from you soon on this subject, as I shall leave home on or before the first of next month, and wish to give particular directions to the workmen before I go. I am, etc.

Tench Tilghman's reply and his accompanying sketch are prime documents in the history of the development of orangeries in America. On the eighteenth of the month he replied:

Inclosed you will find answers to your Several Queries respecting the Green House including the order in which they were put, and that you may the better understand the Construction of Mrs Carroll's, I have made a rough Plan of the Manner of conducting the Flues — Your Floor being 40 feet long Mrs Carroll recommends two Flues to run up the Back Wall, because you may then increase the number of Flues which run under the Floor, and which she looks upon as essential — The trees are by that means kept warm at the Roots — She does not seem to think there is any occasion for the Heat to be conveyed all around the Walls by means of small Vacancies left in them She has always found the Flues mark'd in the plan sufficient for her House —

She recommends it to you to have the upper parts of your Window sashes to pull down, as well as the lower ones to rise — you then Give Air to the Tops of your Trees —

Your Ceiling she thinks ought to be Arched and at least 15 feet high — She has found the lowness of hers which is but 12 very inconvenient —

Smooth Stucco she thinks preferable to common Plaster because drier —

The Door of the House to be as large as you can conveniently make it — otherwise when the Trees come to any size, the limbs are broken and the Fruit torn off by moving in and out

It is the Custom in many Green Houses to set the Boxes upon Benches — But Mrs Carroll says they do better upon the Floor, because they then receive the Heat from the Flues below to more advantage —

I recollect nothing more — I hope your Excellency will understand this imperfect description of a matter which I do not know much about myself.

This radiant, gravity hot air heating system with the hot air ducts entirely under the floor was considered to be an improvement over an earlier system in which the hot air ducts ran only under the windows and up the north wall in an inclined flue. The earliest section of the orangery at Wye House in Talbot County, constructed in the mid-eighteenth century, utilized this earlier method.[2]

Mrs. Washington had an opportunity to see Mrs. Carroll's orangery when she was entertained at Mount Clare while traveling to New York for her husband's first inauguration. Robert Lewis, a nephew of the president-elect, accompanied his aunt, and his diary for May 19, 1789 describes the visit:

> M[rs] Carroll Expecting M[rs] W — had made considerable preparation, — we found a large bowl of salubrious ice punch with fruits &c. which had been plucked from the trees in a green House lying on the tables in great abundance; — these after riding 25 or 30 miles without eating or drinking was no unwelcome luxury, however, M[rs] C — could not complain that we had not done her punch honor, for in the course of 1 Quarter of an Hour . . . this bowl which held upwards of two Gallons was entirely consumed to the no little satisfaction of us all. —

Margaret Tilghman Carroll's letters to Washington have not survived, but she evidently offered to provide orange trees for the new orangery of Mount Vernon. Four months after his wife's visit, the President wrote to Mrs. Carroll:

New York, September 16, 1789

> Mdam: A Person having been lately sent to me from Europe in the capacity of a Gardner, who professes a knowledge in the culture of rare plants and care of a Green-House, I am desirous to profit of the very obliging offer you were pleased some time ago to make me.
> In availing myself of your goodness I am far from desiring that it should induce any inconvenience to yourself. but, reconciling your disposition to oblige, with your convenience, I shall be happy to receive such aids as you can well spare, and as will not impair your collection. Trusting that this will be rule of your bounty, I have requested General Williams to give you notice, when an opportunity offers to transport the trees or plants in the freshest state to Mount Vernon, and to pay any expence which may be incurred in fitting them for transportation, and to receive them from your Gardner for that purpose. I have the honor etc.

In early October Washington wrote to General Otho Holland Williams in Baltimore saying: "I have reason to fear that my request of you to forward the plants which Mrs. Carroll had been so obliging as to offer me was so incautiously expressed, as to lead you into a mistake, and myself consequently into an expence which I had no intention to incur."

The President had expected that several small orange trees would be sent on the packet boat from Baltimore to Alexandria. He now realized that Mrs. Carroll was making a gift of her largest trees which would require chartering a vessel to transport the trees to Mount Vernon. The correspondence continued with another letter from Mrs. Carroll hoping that the President would accept the trees from her orangery. Washington replied on October 14:

> My Green House is by no means in perfect order, and if it was, it would not have been my wish to have robbed yours of any *grown* or bearing plants. If it is not too late, I would again repeat and entreat that this may not happen.
> Mrs. Washington joins me in thanking you for your polite invitation to Mount Clare (on the supposition that we should return to Virginia during the recess of Congress).

but went on to say that Mrs. Washington and he would be touring the eastern states instead of returning to Mount Vernon for the recess. Finally, in late November, the President wrote Otho Williams: "I can no longer refuse the kind and pressing offer of bearing fruit Trees from the good

Lady," and to Mrs. Carroll: "I am overcome by your goodness, and shall submit to your decision with respect to the plants from your Green House." He went on to say: " . . . from some late accounts of the alteration my new Gardner has been making at Mount Vernon . . . my Green House will be completely in order for them."

In addition to the orangery, Margaret Carroll also maintained a greenhouse at Mount Clare. This 24 by 39 foot structure was to the west of the orangery and linked with it by a brick wall. There was a balancing dependency of the same size to the east of the wash house, described in the 1798 Federal Direct Tax only as a "shed." With the addition of these two outbuildings, the garden elevation of Mount Clare extended over 350 feet along its hilltop.[3]

It not known whether the greenhouse was constructed before the Revolution or after. The earliest extant reference to it is in the 1798 Tax description of the property, and the earliest view is in a lithograph of Mount Clare made in 1862 which shows the greenhouse in a deteriorated condition.

The Barrister's copy of the 1759 edition of Miller's *The Gardeners Dictionary* described the construction of greenhouses, or "stoves" as they were then termed. Miller recommended that the section of the stove containing the plants be approximately 12 feet deep with a work shed behind it to give some measure of insulation from the north winds. The sloping glass wall of the stove should start about three feet above the ground and rise a maximum of 16 feet. As with some orangeries, the heating flues of eighteenth century greenhouses ran up the tall north wall at a shallow incline with six or eight turns.

Although Peale's landscape of 1775 does not show the greenhouse, this cannot be used as positive evidence that it was not constructed by that time since the architectural backgrounds in other works by Peale indicate that he used artistic license in altering buildings to suit his compositional needs.

Mrs. Ambler, on her tour of the gardens at Mount Clare in 1770, remarked upon the 100 pineapple plants that were being grown. According to Miller's *Dictionary*, these could be raised in a greenhouse the size of the Carrolls'. The pineapples could also have been grown in a cold frame. What may prove to be the foundations of a cold frame has been found between the orangery and the ogee roofed shed to its east.[4]

About the same time Washington was writing about his orangery, Mrs. Carroll was making a number of alterations to Mount Clare to update its appearance and to make the house more convenient. After the American Revolution, with the return to normal life and the revival of business and trade, a surge of building activity swept the nation and Mrs. Carroll's changes were a part of this tide of activity. The alterations in the new Federal style reflect not only the eclipse of Annapolis by Baltimore as a fashion center but also the change of Mount Clare from the country house of a man with important financial and political activities to the year-round residence of a woman whose house was a center of hospitality in the fast-growing city.

In addition to stylistic evidence, the changes can be dated by an advertisement which appeared in the October 6, 1789 issue of the *Maryland Journal:*

> Kennedy, Joseph, Stucco-workman, Plasterer, and Plain-Painter, from Dublin, Has settled in Baltimore, and may be seen at Mr. Collins's, on Howard's-Hill: He will undertake to perform the several Branches of his Profession, in the most approved and latest Fashions — Having been regularly bred under as good Workmen as any in Ireland, he flatters himself, that he shall be able to satisfy those who may employ him. A Specimen of his Work may be seen at Mount-Clare, near Town.

The work can also be dated by changes Charles Willson Peale made to Mrs. Carroll's portrait. Peale's day book records that he altered the painting in June 1788. Recent x-rays taken by the conservation department of the Walters Art Gallery reveal that Margaret Carroll had her hair changed from a tightly pulled back pompadour to a style that was fuller at the sides and that she had the spray of orange leaves in her right hand altered. In addition, Peale changed the circular window in the pediment of the garden front of the house, in the background of the portrait, to the new lunette window Mrs. Carroll had installed. The lunette window, set within a segmental arch, was divided into three sections by wood mullions. This design is known as a Diocletian window and was widely used in the Federal and early Greek Revival periods in America. Mount Clare's was among the earliest examples in the Baltimore area. This larger window in the pediment, reusing the original keystone, was a small change, but it evidently satisfied Margaret Carroll's desire to modernize the forty year old garden facade.

Eight foot wide service passages were added to the far side of each wing sometime before 1798, and it is thought that Mrs. Carroll had these built at the time she was making her other alterations. Moving the service entrances farther from the main house reflected the growing desire to separate service functions from family and entertainment areas. The concept of privacy between servants and family, as well as between family members, grew in importance throughout the eighteenth century. Appearing in English and Continental planning first, it did not generally affect American residential architecture until after the Revolution. The service stair added to Mount Clare in the late 1760's was an early example in Maryland of this concept and the service passages were a continuation of this desire for privacy.

The call bells in Mount Clare were probably installed at the time of Mrs. Carroll's other changes. Bells connected by a series of wires to pulls in the principal rooms of houses were a technical development of the later part of the eighteenth century which permitted further privacy for both families and their servants. At Mount Clare, the board holding the bells, with a bell of different tone for each room, was most likely mounted in the passage in the kitchen wing.

Mrs. Carroll also had a larder constructed off the hyphen between the dining room and the kitchen wing. The room that had been called the scullery was now referred to as the pantry. Since it had a fireplace, it probably was used as a servants' hall as well.

The original exterior entrance to the basement was blocked by the new larder so the bulkhead containing the steps down to the basement was moved to the east wall of the addition and a passage with brick walls and floor constructed under the new room connecting the relocated bulkhead to the basement.

Inside the house, Margaret Carroll restricted her alterations to replacing the mid-Georgian mantels with new ones in the Federal style. These were probably the work of Joseph Kennedy. In the parlor and dining room, the mantels contained composition ornament of very fine quality. Two even finer mantels, an "unmatched pair," were installed in the rooms in the former office wing. The former clerk's bedchamber probably continued in use as a bedchamber, and the Barrister's office was changed into a drawing room. Since this was now one of the important rooms for entertaining guests Kennedy may also have added decorative plasterwork to the ceiling. The creation of a high-style drawing room gave Mrs. Carroll the three rooms which were considered necessary in the late eighteenth century for large entertainments: one for dining, one for cards, and one for dancing.[5]

The only two mantels not changed at this time were those in Mrs. Carroll's bedchamber and in the room which for a few years had been her daughter's. Both the Barrister and his wife were consistently style-conscious and the only apparent break in this pattern was Mrs. Carroll's decision to keep the mantels in these two rooms. Perhaps the rooms held too many memories for her.

In 1798 a Federal Direct Tax was made of all the taxable property in the United States. By this

Parlor mantel. Wood with composition ornament, 64¼ inches high by 73½ inches wide. One of the mantels installed during the changes made by Mrs. Carroll circa 1788. This mantel may be part of the work referred to by Joseph Kennedy in his advertisement in the October 6, 1789 issue of the *Maryland Journal*. *Photograph by Duane Suter.*

time Margaret Carroll had completed her alterations to Mount Clare, and it is interesting to compare the taxable value of her house with others in Maryland. Mount Clare was taxed at $5,000 and the house on Green Street in Annapolis, now occupied by the Nicholas Carrolls, at $1,650. The Ridout house in Annapolis was valued at $1,400, the Hammond-Harwood house at $1,800 and the Chase-Lloyd house at $2,500. Whitehall in Anne Arundel County was taxed at $1,200 and Belair in Prince George's County was $2,250. Belvidere, the large and stylish house which Governor John Eager Howard had recently completed on the outskirts of Baltimore, was listed at $4,000.

Dining room mantel. Wood with composition ornament. 63¼ inches high by 73½ inches wide. This mantel is another of those thought to have been made by Joseph Kennedy and installed when Mrs. Carroll made her changes to the house circa 1788. *Photograph by Duane Suter.*

Charles Carroll, Barrister's estate descended by inheritance to two of his nephews, Nicholas and James (Maccubbin) Carroll, each of whom controlled the assets of his own portion, paying half of the income to their uncle's widow.

James Carroll, who would ultimately inherit Mount Clare, moved from Annapolis to Baltimore sometime after 1785. In December 1787, he married Sophia Gough, the only child of Harry Dorsey Gough, at that time the wealthiest man in Baltimore. The wedding took place at Perry Hall, the Gough's country house 14 miles north of Baltimore. James's father, Nicholas Maccubbin, died the year of James's marriage, leaving him two plantations totaling over 1,300 acres on the Rhode River in Anne Arundel County. One was Squirrel Neck with the house that had influenced the design of Mount Clare's garden facade. James also inherited his parents' house in Annapolis, which Dr. Carroll had built in the 1720's.

The James Carrolls may have used the Annapolis house while James served in the Lower House and the Senate of the state legislature between 1787 and 1799. After 1803 the Carrolls were listed in the Baltimore directories as living at 83 Front Street, the address of Harry Dorsey Gough's town house. They also spent considerable time with Sophia Carroll's parents in the country at Perry Hall. After Mr. Gough's death in 1808, his widow gave up the house in Baltimore, and the Carrolls maintained a residence at Greene and Saratoga Streets.

James added to the acreage of Mount Clare and in 1812 had the property resurveyed to include the parcels of land he had purchased. The survey took ten pages to describe the boundaries of Mount Clare, which now totaled 1,005.5 acres. The new survey also legally changed the name of the property from "part of Georgia" to "Mount Clare."

Nicholas Carroll inherited the far greater portion of his uncle's estate. Shortly after the Barrister's death, he married Ann Jennings of Annapolis and moved into the Carroll house on Green Street. From his father, Nicholas inherited about 800 acres on the South River in Anne Arundel County as well as a 1,000 acre plantation across the Bay in Kent County which he had been managing prior to his father's death.

Nicholas Carroll continued his uncle's farming operations at The Caves in Baltimore County, but did not maintain a residence there. Margaret Carroll, however, had a house at The Caves. The 1798 Federal Direct Tax description of the property lists a one story, 24 foot by 24 foot, frame, octagonal dwelling with a detached stone kitchen. The inventory of Margaret Carroll's property at the time of her death lists the furniture in this house and indicates that it had no more than three rooms. There are no surviving records to determine whether Mrs. Carroll built this interestingly shaped "pavillion" or if she and her husband had used it earlier. From the furnishings inventoried, one can surmise that it was probably used as a retreat in the hot summer months.

As the nineteenth century opened, the wooded hills to the north of Mount Clare began to be dotted with the country seats of Baltimore merchants who were amassing great fortunes in shipping, trade, and banking. Their houses were often designed in the fashionable neo-classical style and sited so that from the windows and lawns there were views of the city with its harbor below in the distance. Next to Mount Clare was Willow Brook, the 26 acre estate of John Donnell. Across the Frederick Road were the Robert Gilmores at Beach Hill, and next to them was Harlem, built by Adrian Valch. Harlem was noted for its especially fine and extensive gardens, which contained an orangery.[6]

The comfortable routine of life at Mount Clare was shattered in the late summer of 1814. Two years earlier, hostilities had begun between the United States and Great Britain in what would later be known as the War of 1812. Up to 1814, as far as Baltimore was concerned, the war had been confined to the water, but in August of that year British troops disembarked in Southern Maryland and made their way toward Washington.

   Mantel in study. Wood with composition ornament, 59½ inches high by 64¼ inches wide. The top shelf is a late nineteenth or early twentieth century addition. The study is the smallest room on the first floor and the size of the mantel and the delicacy of its detail reflect the scale of the room. This mantel also dates from the period of Margaret Tilghman Carroll's alterations to Mount Clare. *Photograph by Duane Suter.*

The highway past Mount Clare's gates must have been alive with couriers riding between the capital and Baltimore. On August 22, units of the Maryland militia marched past Mrs. Carroll's, first to bivouac at Elk Ridge and then on to Bladensburg. James Carroll, Jr., on duty with the militia, was among the troops passing Mount Clare toward battle.

The British swept over the Americans at Bladensburg and on into Washington. On the night of the twenty-fourth James Carroll, Jr., while riding back to Baltimore with dispatches, heard the

Mantel installed by Mrs. Margaret Carroll in the bed chamber in the west wing. Wood with composition ornament. The mantel in the wing drawing room matched this except for a few richer details and a more elaborate center motif containing allegorical figures. These mantels are believed to have been made by Joseph Kennedy. Plate 18 of *Architecture, Furniture, and Interiors of Maryland and Virginia During the Eighteenth Century* by Newton W. Elwell. *Photograph by the Hughes Company.*

explosions as the Capitol was blown up. In the city that night, the southwestern sky glowed red from the fires in Washington forty miles away.

Defeated troops poured up the road past Mount Clare toward Baltimore. The British army, back on its transports, was also headed for Baltimore, with the avowed purpose of destroying the city they termed a "nest of pirates." As the fleet entered the mouth of the Patapsco River on Sunday, September 11, the ships would have been clearly visible from the lawn of Mount Clare. An even better view could have been obtained from an upstairs window with the aid of the Barrister's spyglass.

James (Maccubbin) Carroll (1761-1832) by Thomas Edge Pine, (1730?-1788), circa 1787. Oil on Canvas, 34 by 28 inches. *Private collection.*

Sophia Gough Carroll (1730?- 1816), twentieth century, by Richard Pultenay. Copy of painting by Thomas Edge Pine, (1730-1788), circa 1787. Oil on canvas, 30 by 25 inches. *Collection of Mrs. William C. Stettinius, Photograph courtesy of the Frick Art Reference Library.*

Because the city's defenders had sunk a row of ships to block the Northwest Branch of the river, which led to the harbor, and another row across the Middle Branch, beyond which lay Mount Clare, the British could not reach the city by ship. They were forced instead to disembark their troops at North Point, at the mouth of the Patapsco. On September twelfth, 4,700 troops landed and marched up the North Point Road toward Baltimore. The American forces, entrenched on Hampstead Hill on the eastern outskirts of the city, engaged the enemy and stopped its advance.

The next day, the British naval force began its bombardment of Fort McHenry, on Whetstone Point at the mouth of the harbor, two miles to the southeast of Mount Clare. The British land forces were being beaten back, and the bombardment, originally planned as part of a joint action, was now a last effort. From her house on its hilltop, Margaret Carroll must have watched the attack on the fort in the distance with even greater emotion than most of the other citizens of Baltimore. All that her husband and her father had striven for during the Revolutionary War, forty years before, hung in the balance. The bombardment lasted all day and through the night until 4 A.M. when, just before dawn, the British guns fell silent.

Then the British retreated. The fleet moved out to the mouth of the river and the troops re-embarked. On September fifteenth, the British fleet sailed down the Chesapeake Bay and out into the Atlantic. Baltimore was saved.

In January 1817 Mrs. Carroll celebrated her seventy-fifth birthday, but she was far from well. On March twelfth she began her will, adding a long codicil to it the next day. Two days later, on March 15, 1817, Margaret Tilghman Carroll died at Mount Clare. As she had requested, she was buried in the Carroll vault in St. Anne's churchyard in Annapolis.

Mrs. Carroll had been a very well-to-do woman. By the terms of her will, the bulk of her estate passed to her nephew Tench Tilghman, Jr., to her niece Elizabeth Tench Goldsborough, and to one of her husband's nephews, Henry Brice, who for a number of years had acted as her business agent. She also made a bequest to the "female charity school attached to St. Paul's Church," where she had been a communicant for over forty years. In addition to flatware and some plated ware, Mrs. Carroll left 890 ounces of silver which she divided among her sister, her niece and James Carroll. She specifically left her largest silver waiter to one of her husband's great-nieces, Margaret Clare Brice Smith, who had been named for the Carrolls' daughter shortly after Margaret Clare Carroll had died. Mrs. Carroll's jewelry was given to her niece. Among the pieces was a ring containing a miniature of Charles I. Margaret Carroll had inherited the ring from her mother, Ann Lloyd Tilghman, who had received it from her grandmother, Henrietta Maria Neale, a godchild of Queen Henrietta Maria. In addition to silver, James Carroll was left the contents of the drawing room in the west wing and of the orangery. To her executors, Tench Tilghman, Jr. and Henry Brice, Mrs. Carroll bequeathed her 47 slaves with directions that they be freed at such ages when they could take care of themselves. She further directed that her executors provide "for the comfortable support of the aged and infirm" among them.

The inventory of the contents of Mount Clare made at the time of Margaret Carroll's death reveals the scale of living she enjoyed as well as the changes in taste which had occurred during the period of her widowhood. There was now stair carpeting, held by 22 stair rods. Brussels carpets were on the floors of the first floor rooms. The carpet in the dining room was overlaid by an oil cloth rug. (It was the usual practice at the time to protect a valuable carpet in a dining room from scuffs from shoes and crumbs of food with a baize or oil cloth rug which could be taken up when entertainments were held). The pair of mirrors with branches for candles ordered for the parlor by the Barrister in 1760 still hung between the windows of that room. But now the parlor was called the drawing room and the mirrors were listed as girandoles in the inventory. In addition, over the mantel in the drawing room was a large looking glass. The two "Lolls" or lolling chairs, which came into fashion early in the nineteenth century, listed as being on the first floor of the house, were most likely in this room also.

The contents of the drawing room which Mrs. Carroll created out of her husband's office were listed separately. The list is interesting both for reason of what the room contained and for the value given them in 1817.

In the wing Drawing Room:

1	Brussels Carpet and hearth Rug	140
1	Lisbon Do	25
12	Arm Chairs and two Sophas	35
2	pier Tables	30
1	marble Slab	25
1	print of Gen. Washington &	
2	paintings	15
1	Mahogany Breakfast Table	7.50
1	pair of And Irons shovel tongs and Brushes	22.50
1	Tea Table and Stand	8
3	Sets of Lusters and 3 Brackets	40
3	window Curtains drapery and pins	150
14	Dimithy Chair covers	21

The two "paintings" are the only ones listed in the house and possibly were the portraits of the Barrister and Mrs. Carroll painted by Charles Willson Peale in 1771. (Two "Landscapes" which were listed in Mrs. Carroll's bed chamber are believed to be the two of Mount Clare that Peale painted in 1775.) The curtains, with their high value, would have been elaborately hung in the height of fashion, similar to those illustrated in *A Collection of Designs for Household Furniture and Interior Decoration in the Most Approved and Elegant Taste*, published in London in 1808 by "George Smith, Upholder Extraordinary to His Royal Highness the Prince of Wales," a book widely used on both sides of the Atlantic. The value assigned to the curtains is in contrast to that given to the twelve chairs and two sofas. These comprised the suite of white and gilt painted Louis XV furniture purchased by Margaret Carroll. There are no surviving records to show where or when the furniture was purchased. Neither is there any hint as to how it happened to be in this country. This elegant French furniture, unexpected in an American house at this period, shows that Mrs. Carroll, with her eye for style, was not afraid to go outside the mainstream of contemporary taste when the occasion merited.

When Margaret Tilghman Carroll came to Mount Clare in 1763 as a bride, the house had been completed only a few years. For 54 years—34 of them as a widow—she was the mistress of Mount Clare. Clearly the house and its gardens bore the stamp of her personality and reflected her taste. With her death, the first great era of Mount Clare ended.

Mount Clare in 1862, seen from the northwest. Detail of a colored lithograph "CAMP CARROLL, BALTIMORE, MD. Lith. & Print. by E. Sachse & Co. 104 S. Charles St. Balto. Ent. . . .1862 by E. Sachse & Co. . . . Maryland". The mansion is seen behind the 13th Calvary Regiment, Pennsylvania Volunteers riding in review. The wings and forecourt walls and orangery are still standing. At the right end is the greenhouse in ruins. At this time the house and its dependencies were rented to the Sugden family who operated the Mount Camp Carroll hotel in them. *Collection of the Maryland Historical Society.*

VI

THE NINETEENTH CENTURY

Although James Carroll inherited Mount Clare in 1783, he had to wait until Margaret Carroll's death in 1817 to come into possession of the estate. By that time he was 56 years old and a widower.

His two eldest sons had married and established their own households. In 1811 James, Jr. had married Achsah Ridgely, and four years later his brother, Harry Dorsey Gough Carroll, had married Achsah's sister, Eliza. The two brides were daughters of Charles Ridgely, governor of Maryland from 1815 to 1818. In a situation similar to that of Nicholas and James Carroll, Charles Ridgely, in 1790, had inherited a very sizable fortune from his uncle, Captain Charles Ridgely, upon condition that he change his surname from Carnan to Ridgely.[1] In the complicated relationships among Maryland families, the young men's father-in-law was also their great-uncle. (Their maternal grandmother, Prudence Carnan Gough, was a sister of Governor Ridgely.) The relationship would be repeated again with the marriage of James, Jr.'s and Harry's sister, Prudence Gough Carroll, to their wives' brother, John Ridgely.

James Carroll's extant account books, which begin in 1813, show few entries for furnishings. When he and his wife moved to their own house at Saratoga and Greene Streets, after Mr. Gough's death, the contents of the Goughs' town house on Front Street went with them. In turn, some of these were later absorbed into the existing furnishings at Mount Clare when James moved there in 1817. Among the very few pieces of furniture purchased by James after he moved into Mount Clare were a clock, in 1824, which cost $32.50 plus an additional 50 cents for "removing" it to his house, a rocking chair for $13 in 1826 and a pianoforte for which he paid $101 in 1828.

The account books record that James Carroll had the chimneys at Mount Clare swept regularly and that every nine months he subscribed five dollars to the Washington Hose Company. The bells in the house were repaired in 1821; the following year the kitchen fireplace was relined with brick. A new convenience was added in the kitchen in 1824 with the purchase of a "refrigerator."

James's accounts and letters also record the family's holiday trips. In the early 1820's they visited Bedford Springs in Pennsylvania. Later they also traveled to Warm Springs, Virginia. In

1828 the Carrolls went to the ocean for the first time, to Cape May, and returned on several later occasions.

Although James Carroll had retired from political life by the beginning of the nineteenth century, he remained one of the more prominent men in Baltimore's public life. Upon Lafayette's return visit to the United States in 1824, James was a member of the committee which arranged for the Revolutionary hero's visit to Baltimore in October of that year and was among those who greeted Lafayette when he landed at Fort McHenry. During the visit, Lafayette recalled that James's uncle, Charles Carroll, Barrister, had been one of those who, in 1781, loaned him a much needed $7,256 to purchase supplies for his troops when General Wayne and he had passed through Baltimore with their troops on their way to Yorktown.

In 1815 the Washington Turnpike had been constructed across the pastures below Mount Clare's gardens. The turnpike crossed Gwynns Falls by the Carrolls' grist mill, with a tollgate located on the east side of the falls near the mill. The mill had been enlarged over the years and was now one of the major flour mills in the region. In 1824 one customer alone purchased 9,000 barrels of "super fine flour."

In the late 1820's James Carroll began to expand the industrial development of his property. In 1827 he leased twelve-and-three-quarters acres along the turnpike to Joseph Jameson, William Trimble and Samuel Fenby for digging clay and making bricks. This was the first of a number of brick kilns on the property. By the end of the nineteenth century, over 85 million bricks would be produced from clay dug on Mount Clare land.

In December 1830 Carroll deeded ten acres at the northeast corner of his property to the newly formed Baltimore and Ohio Railroad for a depot. This Mount Clare Station was the first railroad station in the country.[2]

James had wanted the railroad to cross his property below the Washington turnpike but was not successful. Finally, and very reluctantly, he agreed that it could cross to the north of his house. At Gwynns Falls the railroad constructed a 312 foot long stone bridge, known as the Carrollton Viaduct, with a single 100 foot long arch. Built in 1829, it is the oldest railroad bridge in the United States. It was considered an engineering marvel at the time of its construction and is still in daily use. However, the viaduct carrying the railroad over the falls disturbed the millrace for the Mount Clare mill, causing enough irritation for James Carroll to detail the problems of the bridge and the new course of the millrace in his will.

The route of the railroad also cut off Mount Clare from its entrance on the old highway. A new driveway was constructed up to the house from the Washington turnpike, with a gatehouse at the entrance from the pike.

Tax records indicate that James was leasing his house in Annapolis by the late eighteenth century. He also leased Squirrel Neck but farmed the adjacent plantation, The Haylands. The Carroll accounts show that each year produce from The Haylands was sent to Mount Clare for the family's use. The family also raised tobacco, wheat and rye at The Haylands as cash crops and sold butter from the dairy herd there. In 1820 James sold the Annapolis house and in 1825 he sold Squirrel Neck to John Contee.[3] The Carrolls continued their farming operations at The Haylands which was also used by James, Jr. and his family as their summer residence.

James Carroll's income was derived from a number of sources: the mill on Gwynns Falls, the Mount Clare land leased for industrial uses, rents from several houses on Carroll's Point where the family's shipyard had been, and from the plantation on the Rhode River in Anne Arundel County. Additional income came from the rents on the large number of lots and buildings his wife had inherited from her father. When his mother-in-law, Mrs. Gough, died in 1822, James inherited Huntington, comprising 400 acres immediately to the north of Baltimore. This land was

James Carroll, Jr. (1791-1873) by William James Hubard (1807-1862), circa 1832. Oil on wood, 19 by 15 inches. *Collection of Mrs. William C. Stettinius, Photograph courtesy of the Frick Art Reference Library.*

farmed and held for development as the city expanded northward.

By the early nineteenth century the family was investing its capital in new directions, reflecting the expanding economy and early industrial development of the nation. James Carroll owned stock in the Bank of Baltimore, the Union Bank of Baltimore and the Bank of Maryland. He was also a stock-holder in the Reisterstown Turnpike, the Frederick Turnpike, the Susquehanna Canal and, after 1829, the Baltimore and Ohio Railroad.

James Carroll died at Mount Clare on January 27, 1832. At his death he owned approximately 1,400 acres in Baltimore City and Baltimore County which he divided between his sons, James, Jr. and Charles Ridgely Carroll.[4] In addition to lots and buildings in Baltimore City, James, Jr. received 684 acres of Mount Clare. This included the area from the future bed of Nanticoke Street down to the river, and the land east of Gwynns Run between the railroad and the turnpike, in the midst of which sat Mount Clare mansion with its outbuildings.

Mr. and Mrs. James Carroll, Jr., who had been living at 94 West Pratt Street, now moved into Mount Clare. As his father had done in 1817, James Carroll, Jr. augmented the existing contents of Mount Clare with furnishings from his town house. In addition to what they had accumulated during twenty years of marriage, James and Achsah Carroll had, by inheritance and purchase, added a significant number of household items at the time of Governor Ridgely's death in 1829.

Achsah Ridgely Carroll inherited over 280 ounces of silver from her father, each item carefully weighed and listed in the estate papers. The list started with a punch bowl weighing 88 ounces, 5 pennyweight and ended with one teaspoon at six pennyweight. She also received one-seventh of a long list of household linens and bedding ranging from 37 damask tablecloths valued at $370 and 41 pairs of linen sheets at $205, to 14 dusting cloths worth 56 cents and a "bag of little bags" at 30 cents.[5]

When the contents of the Governor's town house were sold in October 1829, James and Achsah Carroll purchased 34 lots of items. From the front parlor they bought:

1	Gold Leaver Watch Seal and Key	$86
2	Brass and glass mantel lamps & branches	75
1	Grand Piano Forte	80
1	Marble Center Table	22
1	Set Tea & Coffee, best China (star Pattern), 54 pieces	48
1	Set Bleu and Gilt China, 64 pieces	31
2	Best cut glass Sugar Dishes	7
2	Best cut Glass Sugar Dishes	6
1	Turkey Carpet	70

all of which would have gone to Mount Clare with them.

In 1833 James, Jr. insured Mount Clare with the Baltimore Equitable Society. The fire insurance policy describes the 73 year old "two story brick Mansion House" as "ancient and well finished in high style according to the custom of that day." The main house was insured for $4,800, each hyphen for $100 and each wing at $600, for a total of $6,200. This was two-thirds of the value of the mansion, the maximum for which the Equitable Society would write a policy.

Achsah Ridgely Carroll (1792-1841) by William James Hubbard (1807-1862), 1832. Oil on wood panel, 7 by 6 inches. *Collection of Mrs. Bartow Van Ness, Jr. Photograph by Duane Suter.*

It was probably the younger James Carrolls who changed the gate posts at the entrance to the forecourt. The earlier wood posts seen in the portrait of the Barrister and the view of the house on several pieces of painted furniture were replaced by the rusticated, cut stone piers which appear in the earliest photographs of the house.

Since his father had sold The Haylands in 1831, James, Jr. had fresh produce and other supplies sent regularly to Mount Clare from his farm, Summerfield, in Baltimore County. James had received the farm on Glenarm Road from his father-in-law at the time of his marriage to Achsah Ridgely. The Carrolls added to its acreage until Summerfield totaled 886 acres. Just as James, Jr. and his wife had been given the use of The Haylands as a summer residence, so James III and his wife, Mary Wethered Ludlow, used Summerfield as a country house after their marriage in 1837. They also maintained town residence at 88 West Pratt Street in the winter.

Occasional glimpses of the social life enjoyed by the Carrolls in the early Victorian period can be found in letters and records of other Baltimore families. On February 2, 1837, Mrs. Benjamin I. Cohn gave a fancy dress ball at her house at Charles and Saratoga Streets. The ball stood out in the memory of those attending for many years. As one of her guests later wrote, "every body was there who is at all in the habit of attending parties." The Carrolls were among the guests, with James dressed in a suit of the Barrister's clothes. This must have been among the clothing in the "5 Trunks containing Court wearing Apparel" in the garret at Mount Clare which Margaret Tilghman Carroll had saved from the years of her marriage before the Revolution.

The menu of a "supper" given by Harry Dorsey Gough Carroll, Jr. a number of years later has survived and was probably similar to those given at Mount Clare during the same period. Twenty people sat down to supper, including the James Carrolls, Jr., and were served:

Terrapin

———

Chicken stuffed with Chestnuts
Peas   Ham   Potatoes

———

Sweet Breads
Filet de beuf aux Champignons
Potatoes
Hominay

———

Crab
Lobster Salad

———

Pate de foie gras

———

Ices

———

Cafe Noir

Like his father, James, Jr. studied law, but did not maintain a practice. In 1816 he was appointed a judge of the Orphans Court and later a Trustee of the Poor. He served as a member of the House of Representatives in the 26th Congress, from 1839 to 1841, as a Democrat. After unsuccessfully trying to become the party's candidate for Governor of Maryland in 1844, he retired from political life. Also as his father had before him, James, Jr. pursued an active business career handling the family's investments. He served as a director of the Baltimore and Ohio Railroad and of the Chesapeake and Ohio Canal Company.

After his wife's death in 1841, James Carroll, Jr. continued to live at Mount Clare. In spite of the encroachments of the city, the immediate setting of the house, surrounded now by 364 acres, remained unchanged. The extensive gardens were still maintained, and the family accounts record the payment each spring and fall for moving the orange and lemon trees and other exotic plants out of and back into the orangery.

But the Carrolls could not stop the inevitable enroachment of the row after row of houses from the north and east of Mount Clare, nor the pressures for the industrial development of their land along the Washington Turnpike and down to the Patapsco River. In 1848 the brothers, James and Charles Carroll, encouraged the Baltimore and Ohio Railroad to lay a branch line down the

West Baltimore Schutzen Association at Mount Clare. Detail of *Baltimore Schutzenhof* by Hunckle, circa 1875. Lithograph on paper. It is thought that this lithograph shows one of the annual festivals of the shooting association. *Private collection.*

path of Nanticoke Street between their portions of the lower end of the Mount Clare estate. The same year, James obtained permission from the Baltimore City Council to bulkhead the shore along Ridgely's Cove and to build a wharf on the line of Warner Street from Ostend Street to Carroll's Point.

Finally, as a widower and with his children marrying and establishing their own households, James decided to move into the city. His account book records the usual $3.00 payment for moving the plants from the orangery to the lawn in the spring of 1850, but they were not moved back. Sometime between the fall of that year and October of the next, James Carroll moved from

North elevation of Mount Clare, circa 1889, from a newspaper illustratration based upon a photograph. The house is shown as it appeared during the time it was leased by the West Baltimore Schutzen Association. The eighteenth century hyphens, wings and out-buildings have been demolished and a two story brick wing attached to the west side of the house. At the east end is what appears to be a porch. The forecourt walls have been demolished and replaced by a rail fence. The earlier nineteenth century stone gateposts are still in place, but the heraldic beasts have been removed. The level of the forecourt has been raised and steps placed between the gateposts. At the top of the steps are ballards which date from the period of the gateposts. *Mount Clare collection.*

Mount Clare to 105 West Monument Street. After ninety years of continued occupancy by the Carroll family, Mount Clare was emptied of the furniture and books and silver with which it had been filled since 1760.

James purchased a pair of three story houses located on the southeast corner of West Monument and Howard Streets, two blocks west of Mount Vernon Place, the heart of the fashionable residential quarter of Baltimore. Other family members lived nearby. His brother, Harry Dorsey Gough Carroll, after selling Perry Hall in 1852, lived at 90 West Monument Street, and his son, James III, had moved to number 94.[6]

Since 1830 the fields and pastures around the house at Mount Clare had been leased, and beginning in October 1852, James Carroll rented the mansion with its surrounding 14 acres. The first tenant was Fisher H. White, and the rent was $25.00 per month. The next tenant was Thomas Atkinson, who had the house from February 1853 until March, 1854. Thomas Donahou followed from April through September of that year.

In October 1854, George Sugden began renting the house. James Carroll's accounts indicate that the Sugden family continued at Mount Clare through May 1869 at the same rent of $25.00 per month. The Baltimore City directory in 1858 listed a Thomas Sugden as the proprietor of the Mount Clare Hotel at Mount Clare while George Sugden was listed as keeping the Stag Hall Tavern at 59 Hanover Street.

During the Civil War the Sugdens remained in Mount Clare, but the pastures to the west of the house were used by the United States Army. The 13th Cavalry Regiment, Pennsylvania Volunteers was posted at Camp Carroll immediately to the west of the house, and the 128th Regiment, New York Volunteers was at Camp Millington along Gwynns Falls to the north of Camp Carroll. In 1863 the First Connecticut Cavalry and in 1864 the First Maryland Cavalry were quartered at Camp Carroll. The Sugden family evidently changed the name of their hotel in the house during the war because the 1867 directory lists George Sugden as proprietor of Mount Camp Carroll.

In November 1870, James Carroll leased the Mount Clare mansion and 15 acres to the West Baltimore Schuetzen Association, one of the numerous social clubs established by German families in Baltimore in the second half of the nineteenth century. Their six year lease established the rent at $800.00 yearly, to be paid quarterly, with the option to purchase the property for $35,000. In addition, the new tenant was obliged to make $4,000 worth of repairs to the property immediately and an additional $15,000 worth within the next three years.

The house had had hard use and few repairs for a long time. A view of Camp Carroll in 1862 shows the mansion in the background with the greenhouse in ruins, but the orangery and wings intact. By 1871 the wings and outbuildings were in such deteriorated condition that they had to be pulled down. A newspaper illustration shows the alterations made by the new tenants. A new two story wing containing pantries and a kitchen was built onto the west end of the house. As happened to many eighteenth century buildings at this period, the original heavy window frames and small paned sashes were replaced with narrow frames and sashes with only four panes instead of nine. At Mount Clare, in the course of changing the frames, the window jambs, which may have contained paneled shutters, were replaced with flush boards. Only the two small windows in the end walls of the portico chamber were not altered and still retain their original frames, sills and sashes, as well as the brick infilling between the heads of their frames and their brick segmental arches.

The forecourt walls were demolished and replaced by a rail fence. The ground level of the forecourt was raised and made into a lawn, and three wide steps, placed between the stone gate piers, rose up to a walk that led to the mansion. The pair of lead heraldic beasts purchased by Charles Carroll, Barrister, in 1757 had been removed by the time the changes were made to the forecourt. In 1889 the two lead lions were still in the possession of the Carroll family, but today no trace of them remains.

The West Baltimore Schuetzen Association used Mount Clare as its club house. The old parlor was turned into a dining room and the original dining room became a bar. To the north of the house, the society erected a bowling alley and a shooting range, and to the west was a dancing pavilion. The lawns around the house were used for picnicking and for the association's annual festivals, the first of which was held at Mount Clare on July 31, 1871.

The shooting club used Mount Clare through the 1880's; its original lease was renewed in 1876 and again in 1883. James Carroll, Jr. died in 1873 and his son, James III, in 1887. The family continued renting the house and grounds until the death of James III's widow the following year. Then, with the large number of heirs to satisfy and the continuing industrial and residential expansion to the southwestern part of the city, it appeared to be only a matter of time before the mansion would be razed and the land given over for building sites.

The late 1880's saw the beginning of the City Beautiful movement, when municipalities throughout the United States developed an awareness of the value of green spaces for fresh air and recreation in our industrial cities. The Park Board of the City of Baltimore, acting under this impetus, was pursuing a policy of expanding the city's park system and in 1890 paid the Carroll heirs $45,000 for approximately 20 acres of the Mount Clare property including the house and the remains of the terraced gardens. The following year further acreage was purchased and later more land was acquired until the newly created Carroll Park totaled 162 acres.[7]

The Park Board had the present slate roof put on the house and replaced the simple eighteenth century barge boards at the gable ends with bracketed ones which matched the cornice. The Board also had the chimneys rebuilt with more elaborate shapes. The floors in the house were repaired where they had suffered from heavy use, and the staircase was partially rebuilt. The eighteenth century ice house was filled in, and the pump, near the site of the original kitchen, was repaired. The buildings on the grounds added by the Schuetzen Association were removed, and the Carrolls' stable, referred to as "tumbled-down" in the Park report, was demolished. A new stable was built near the recently extended Monroe Street.

On the grounds, the series of garden falls was restored, carriage drives laid out and a program of tree planting begun. At the foot of the old gardens, a large greenhouse and propagation house were constructed.

From the beginning of the creation of Carroll Park, it was planned to demolish the mid-Victorian wing on Mount Clare. In 1895, the Baltimore architect Joseph Evans Sperry prepared drawings for two story hyphens and wings to be added to the house. Mr. Sperry's design consciously attempted to use the details of the main house and is an early example of the revival of interest in American Colonial architecture. The additions, which were to provide offices for the Park Board at the west end and a residence for the superintendent of Carroll Park at the east end, were not built and for the next ten years the mansion was used by the superintendent and his family.

In 1908 the later wing was finally razed, and the one story hyphens and wings which are presently on the house were built to plans prepared by the architectural firm of Wyatt and Nolting. By coincidence, Mr. Wyatt and Mr. Sperry had been partners for several years in the mid-1880's. The 1908 design incorporated elements of the earlier one and also carefully used details found in the original house. A comparison of the published south elevation of the 1895 design with Wyatt and Nolting's illustrates how far the Colonial Revival had progressed in a decade and how much better the architectural profession now understood eighteenth century proportions. The new construction provided storage areas in the added basements and public facilities for the park on the first floors, while the house remained as the superintendent's residence.[8]

In 1917, a century after the death of Margaret Tilghman Carroll, the National Society of the Colonial Dames of America in the State of Maryland arranged with the City of Baltimore to open Mount Clare to the public as a museum dedicated to Maryland's eighteenth century cultural history. With the advent of the Colonial Dames, the house took on a new life and purpose, becoming the first historic house museum in Maryland. Since that date, Mount Clare has been under the custody of the Colonial Dames, who maintain it jointly with the city's Department of Recreation and Parks.

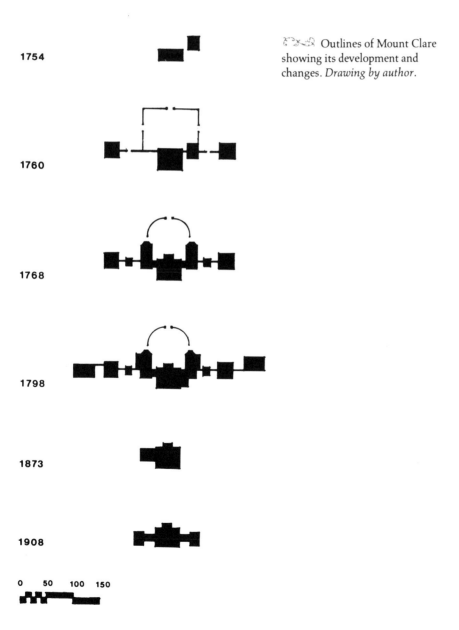

Outlines of Mount Clare showing its development and changes. *Drawing by author.*

Charles Carroll of Carrollton house, Annapolis, Maryland. Lithograph by Edward Sachse (1804-1873), 2 by 3 inches. This earliest recorded view of the Signer's house in Annapolis appeared as in inset in Sachse's *View of Annapolis* published in 1850. *Photograph by Marion E. Warren.*

VII

OTHER HOUSES

Just as several houses had influenced the design of Mount Clare, so in turn Mount Clare influenced a number of later ones. From the time of the Palladian additions in 1768, through the early years of the nineteenth century, Mount Clare was among the most stylish and best known houses in Maryland.

Montpelier in Prince George's County is one of the houses which shows the influence of the Palladian additions on Mount Clare. Sometime between his coming of age in 1772 and the outbreak of the American Revolution, Thomas Snowden began a series of changes to the house he had inherited at the time of his father's death in 1770. Thomas's father had constructed the house about 15 years previously on the family's plantation near their ironworks. The Snowdens were another of the Maryland families whose wealth came from iron furnaces. In 1774 Thomas Snowden married Ann Ridgely, the daughter and heiress of Henry Ridgely of Montpelier in upper Anne Arundel County. Snowden renamed his estate Montpelier for his wife in memory of her father's plantation on which she had grown up. Most probably the alterations to Montpelier were begun shortly after the Snowdens' marriage.

New office and kitchen wings were built on each side of the existing house and connected to it by hyphens. The one story brick wings were constructed with polygonal ends similar to those on Mount Clare. The windows were smaller than those in the Mount Clare wings, and there was a small dormer in the attic of each wing on Montpelier; otherwise the polygonal ends of the wings on the two houses were very similar. Considering the closeness of colonial society in Maryland and the similar business interests of the Snowdens and the Carrolls, it is more than reasonable to believe that Thomas Snowden was inspired by the recently completed work at Mount Clare when he had the new wings designed for his house.

Unlike those at Mount Clare, the wings with their polygonal ends are still standing at Montpelier. Today, the house, located on Route 195 near Laurel, is owned by the National Capital Park and Planning Commission and the grounds are open to the public. Visitors to Montpelier should also notice the octagonal pavilion in the gardens, one of the rare survivals of colonial garden architecture.

The design of the wing Charles Carroll of Carrollton began adding to his father's house in Annapolis in 1770 had a very close relationship to the changes Charles Carroll, Barrister, had just completed at Mount Clare. Charles Carroll, Barrister, and Charles Carroll of Carrollton, 15 years younger than the Barrister, had an unusual number of similarities and connections in their lives. Both were sons of men named Charles Carroll, both families held equal interests in the Baltimore

Company, both men were educated abroad and studied law at the Middle Temple. They were close friends and leaders of the Revolution in Maryland. Their families' houses in Annapolis were "just around the corner" from each other. Each house was one-and-a-half stories with a gambrel roof and they had the same plan.

Charles Carroll of Carrollton's wing, really a separate residence, was larger than the existing house and a full two stories tall. The house and its large wing, connected by an enclosed passage, sat well back on the property, with a walled forecourt separating them from Duke of Gloucester Street. At the entrance of the new wing was a portico with two stone columns. Above the portico was a chamber with a Venetian window in its main facade. Although somewhat smaller than the portico and chamber at Mount Clare, and also simpler in detail, Charles Carroll of Carrollton's portico and chamber were clearly derived from the Barrister's.

The new additions to Mount Clare would have been familiar to the Charles Carroll of Carrollton family. Charles Carroll of Annapolis, Carrollton's father, and Mrs. Rachel Darnall, his mother-in-law, are known to have been house guests at Mount Clare. Undoubtedly Charles Carroll of Carrollton and his wife were entertained there also. With many interconnections already existing between the two Carroll families, the younger Carroll added another by repeating on his own house one of the outstanding design elements of Mount Clare.

Although Charles Carroll of Carrollton's wing was demolished a century ago, it is known through two views drawn by Edward Sachse in the decade before the Civil War. The Sachse views show the original house after it had been enlarged to a full two stories late in the eighteenth century. The nine foot passage connecting the two sections of the house, the same length as the hyphens at Mount Clare, is also indicated as being the full height of the house. To the left in the Sachse illustrations, beyond the forecourt wall, is the large porch on the Carrollton wing which overlooked the still extant garden falls and from which the family had a view across Carroll's Creek (now Spa Creek) to the Chesapeake Bay beyond.

Joseph Evans Sperry, in discussing his design for new hyphens and wings for Mount Clare in 1895, called attention to the similarities between that house and the Hammond-Harwood house in Annapolis. Designed in 1773 by William Buckland, the Hammond-Harwood house is a generation later than Mount Clare. As a result it shows a more polished, late-Colonial detailing than the earlier house, but as Mr. Sperry pointed out, their "design outline's" are "not unlike." Both houses have the basic Annapolis regional plan with a short entrance passage, the stair to one side and the major first floor room on the garden side extending across the center axis of the house. On the entrance front of the Hammond-Harwood House, the wings project beyond the face of the main house and have polygonal ends, which is identical to the arrangement and design at Mount Clare. On their garden facades, both houses have giant pilasters and a central pediment.

It is interesting to compare the pilasters on Squirrel Neck, built circa 1748, Mount Clare, completed in 1760, and the Hammond-Harwood house, designed in 1773. The differences among them reflect the increasing technical ability of the craftsmen as well as the knowledge of their designers. At Squirrel Neck, the pilasters have simply molded brick capitals which sit directly under the cornice. Academically, there should be a frieze and an architrave between the capital and the cornice. At Mount Clare the capitals are more elaborate, using five courses of molded bricks, but they still sit incorrectly under the cornice. When Charles Willson Peale painted Mrs. Margaret Tilghman Carroll in 1771, using the garden facade of Mount Clare as the background of the portrait, he painted a correct entablature on the house, something which it has never had. Finally, on the Hammond-Harwood house, Buckland designed a correct entablature with the capitals of the pilasters supporting a frieze and architrave under the cornice.

Hope House, Talbot County, Maryland. This photograph of the entrance front, taken about 1860, shows the house as built by Tench and Margaret Tilghman in the early nineteenth century. In 1905 the hyphens and wings were greatly enlarged. *Photograph courtesy of Mr. the late and Mrs. W. Flaccus Stifel.*

There is no evidence that William Buckland ever worked at Mount Clare, but he must have seen it. There are too many similarities between the Barrister's house overlooking the Patapsco and the one Buckland designed in Annapolis to be coincidental. Matthias Hammond, who commissioned Buckland to design his Annapolis residence, would have known Mount Clare through his friendship with Charles Carroll, Barrister. Hammond could well have arranged for his architect to visit the Barrister's house, which he evidently admired. And Buckland, the finest

105

pre-Revolutionary architect in Maryland, with a superb eye for design, transposed the several ideas into his own composition with impeccable proportions and detailing.

Hope House, on the Wye River in Talbot County, is related to Mount Clare both by architectural design and by ownership. Throughout the eighteenth century, the Lloyd and Tilghman families were connected by numerous marriages. In the 1730's Robert Lloyd of Hope married Anna Maria Tilghman. Their daughter, Deborah, married Peregrine Tilghman and, in time, Robert's grandson, Tench Tilghman, inherited Hope. This Tench had been named for his father's famous cousin, Colonel Tench Tilghman, General Washington's aide-de-camp. In the early nineteenth century, the younger Tench married Margaret Tilghman, a daughter of Colonel Tench Tilghman and niece of Mrs. Margaret Tilghman Carroll. All four parents of the young couple were first cousins.

Shortly after Tench and Margaret Tilghman inherited Hope in 1808, they built a new house on the plantation which they then called Hope House. The two-and-a-half story brick house has an advancing center pavilion with an entrance porch supported by four wood Roman Doric columns. Above the porch, on the second floor, is a Palladian window. The plan of the first floor is similar to Mount Clare's with the exception that the parlor and dining room at Hope House are of equal size. The hyphens at Hope House echo those at Mount Clare with ogee roofs curving down from the main house to the one story wings. At the Tilghman house, however, the shape is entirely decorative while at Mount Clare it was used to provide headroom for the service stair. An early photograph of Hope House, taken about 1860, shows the original hyphens and wings before they were rebuilt in 1905.

Margaret Tilghman of Hope House was named for her aunt and it was a complimentary gesture to model the design of the new house after her aunt's, as well as an indication that Mount Clare was still considered to be elegant and high-style in the Federal period.

Winton, in Queen Anne's County, is remembered as having similarly shaped hyphens. The house, built by the Earle family in the Federal period, burned around 1910. Several years later a New York financier purchased the property, built a much larger house on the site, and gave it its present name, Pioneer Point.

In Connecticut are three houses with entrance facades clearly related to the design of Mount Clare's. There was no connection between the architect, whoever he might have been, of the 1768 changes to Charles Carroll, Barrister's house and the architect of the New England examples. The relationship is derived through the original English design source. The three Connecticut buildings: Oldgate in Farmington, and Sheldon's Tavern and the Deming house in Litchfield, were designed by William Spratt. Spratt had been an officer in General Burgoyne's army and was captured at the Battle of Saratoga. While being held a prisoner of war in Connecticut, he married Elizabeth Seelye of Litchfield. William Spratt remained in America after the Revolution and in the 1780's and 90's designed a number of houses in the Litchfield and Farmington areas. All three of these houses are of frame construction and have advancing center pavilions composed of four Ionic columns supporting a clapboarded section above containing a Palladian window. The center pavilions project only the diameter of the columns. The Deming house and Oldgate have false balustrades under their Palladian windows, making them appear closer to the facade in plate 39 of Isaac Ware's *A Complete Body of Architecture* than the other Connecticut example or Mount Clare.

Sheldon's Tavern, Litchfield, Connecticut. The post-Revolutionary residence, which later became a tavern, was built onto the smaller Sheldon house of 1760. The addition was designed by the British-trained builder William Spratt. *H.A.B.S.*

🌸 Entrance front of Mount Clare, circa 1920.

EPILOGUE

Because of the museum function of Mount Clare, made possible by the efforts of the Society of Colonial Dames, the house has received sympathetic maintenance by the City of Baltimore. In 1940 the Victorian window sashes were replaced with smaller paned sashes reflecting the patterns of the original windows. At the same time, the paint which had covered the exterior of the house since the 1870's was removed, revealing the rubbed and gauged window arches and the pattern of glazed header bricks in the pilasters on the garden elevation. With the paint removed, a portion of the original stone arched basement entrance could be seen at the base of the southeast chimney. The outlines of the door openings from the east hyphen to the house—at the first floor, from the service stair to the upper landing of the main stair and to the basement—were also exposed.

In 1960, when the early twentieth century wings were no longer needed by Carroll Park, they were incorporated into the Mount Clare museum. The east wing was altered to the design of John H. Scarff, A.I.A., to represent an eighteenth century kitchen, and in the west wing early nineteenth century Gothic Revival bookcases were installed to accommodate the growing reference and research library. The woodwork came from Ivy Neck, a Murray family plantation near Squirrel Neck on the Rhode River in Anne Arundel County. On the library shelves today are a number of the Barrister's and Mrs. Carroll's books.

Dining Room at Mount Clare, circa 1930.

In October 1970 Ivor Noel Hume, director of Colonial Williamsburg Foundation's Department of Archaeology, was invited to Mount Clare to investigate an opening in the southeast corner of the basement. Mr. Hume found an eighteenth century drain leading away from the house toward the south. The drain was approximately 28 inches wide and 28 inches high. It had a dirt floor and brick sides terminating in a pointed arch for strength to support the weight of earth above it. On that occasion it was not possible to investigate more than a few feet of the drain so its entrance was closed to await a detailed study in the future.

The next spring Dr. Elizabeth Ralph of the University Museum at the University of Pennsylvania came to Mount Clare with resitivity equipment to investigate the east ends of the bowling green and the garden falls and the lawn east of the house. This equipment, widely used in Europe since 1945, is a non-destructive method of searching for buried building foundations. The report from Dr. Ralph's visit indicated evidence of the drain leading a short distance from the

Parlor at Mount Clare, circa 1930.

house and of possible foundations in the area of the demolished ice house.

During the summer of 1977 Dr. Ralph returned to demonstrate the use of her resitivity equipment to members of the Baltimore County Chapter of the Archaeological Society of Maryland. She graciously loaned the equipment to the society, which found indications of buried foundations to the west of the house where the orangery had stood.

The results of the Baltimore County Chapter's investigations encouraged the Colonial Dames to engage Dr. Nina Poe Zouck to begin an archaeological "dig" in the area indicated by the resitivity meter soundings west of the library wing. In the late summer of 1977 Dr. Zouck undertook a brief dig with several helpers, uncovering a large number of artifacts. The following year Dr. Zouck returned with her students from the University of Maryland Baltimore County Campus. That summer the foundations of the orangery, the small outbuilding between the orangery and office wing, the forecourt wall, and the kitchen were partially excavated.

After Dr. Zouck's move to New England, Norma Baumgartner-Wagner was engaged to continue the archaeological study. During the summer of 1979, the office wing and more of the forecourt walls were discovered by the archaeological team. Portions of the area of the carriage circle were also studied. The 1980 season was spent completing the excavation of the office wing during which traces of the west hyphen were also unearthed.

With the realization of the great extent of the buried remains of the wings and outbuildings, and with the wealth of artifacts being uncovered, it is hoped that Mount Clare will become a major site for the archaeological study of plantation life in the Tidewater area of Maryland.

Over the years during which the National Society of the Colonial Dames of America in the State of Maryland has administered Mount Clare, the collections in the house have been constantly augmented to reflect the life enjoyed by the Barrister and his wife. More and more of the furniture and other objects used by the Carrolls have been returned to the house. In a number of cases a piece of furniture or silver is known to be the exact item ordered in one of Charles Carroll's invoices to his London agent. Mount Clare is the only eighteenth century museum house in Maryland to contain so many of the daily artifacts of life belonging to the builder of the house and used by his family in that house.

Today, just as it was two centuries ago, Mount Clare is a hospitable and welcoming house. Through the efforts of the members of the Society of Colonial Dames, the house with its collections is an interpretation of the economic and cultural life of Tidewater Maryland during the second half of the eighteenth century and an expression of its continuing tradition.

Gates to forecourt, Mount Clare. *Drawing by author.*

Garden elevation of Mount Clare, circa 1910.

PREFACE

[1] Because of Dr. Charles Carroll's many business interests and the large fortune he was to eventually accumulate, some historians have assumed that he quit the practice of medicine soon after arriving in Maryland. However, the doctor's invoices to his agents in England, from the time of his arrival in Annapolis until shortly before his death, included orders for medicines and glass vials indicating that he did maintain an active medical practice.

CHAPTER I

[1] Nothing is known of Dr. Charles Carroll's youth or schooling or medical training. His earliest extant accounts indicate that he had an established medical practice in Annapolis by 1716. Dr. Carroll in Maryland and his brother, John, in Barbados were examples of the men known as the Wild Geese, sons of the ancient Irish aristocracy who left in the years following the defeat of James II in the Battle of the Boyne to seek their fortunes elsewhere. The Wild Geese have been described as "the cream of the Catholic majority." There were colonies of Irish in France, Spain, Austria and even Russia. Only a few came to Protestant Britain's colonies. Dr. Carroll's sister, Dorothy, was the only child of Charles Carroll of Clonlisk to remain in Ireland.

[2] This was Lot 47 on the Stoddert survey of 1718. In later wills and deeds, it was always referred to as the Post House Lot.

[3] In 1955 the old Carroll house was threatened with demolition but was saved through the efforts of Historic Annapolis, Inc. The house was cut into two sections, moved over a two day period through the center of Annapolis, and reassembled on a new site on the campus of St. John's College. It serves today as administrative offices for the College.

[4] Although Dr. Carroll did not state in his letter where he had intended to place his son in school, it very likely was the Jesuit College at St. Omer near Calais. For several generations in the seventeenth and eighteenth centuries, Irish and English Catholic families sent their sons to that fashionable school. Charles Carroll the Settler in Annapolis had his sons educated at St. Omer and later his grandsons studied there also. After Dr. Carroll became a member of the Church of England, he arranged for a Protestant education for his son at Eton.

[5] Dorothy Blake Carroll died in July 1734 and was buried in the graveyard at her uncle's plantation, Bennett's Point. Her grave is still there, marked by a marble slab. At the top of the slab are carved the Carroll arms impaled with those of the Blake family, surmounted by the Carroll crest. Below the coats-of-arms is the inscription:

Here lyeth Interr'd the Remains of
DOROTHY CARROLL, Daughter of Mr.
Charles Blake of Wye River in the Province of
Maryland, and wife of CHARLES CARROLL,
son of CHARLES CARROLL, Esqr. of Clonlisk in the King's Co. & Kingdom of Ireland.
She was Meek, Prudent and Virtuous,
wanting no good quality that compose a good
Christian, and wise, tender and loveing
Mother and Friend.
Tho' young in years, a Matron in Behavior
and Conduct.
She left issue two sons and one Daughter,
who inherit her Beauty, and to be hoped they
will her Virtues.
She departed this life the 8th day of July
Anno Domini 1734
Aged thirty-one Years, Seven Months and
Twelve Days

[6] Sotterley was the finest house in St. Mary's County in the mid-eighteenth century. It is known for its richly paneled parlor and intricate Chinese Chippendale staircase, and for its superb view over the Patuxent River. Located on Route 245 near Hollywood, Maryland, the house is open to the public through the courtesy of the Sotterley Foundation.

[7] Dr. Carroll's correspondent, William Black, had lived in Londontown on the South River — eight miles by road below Annapolis — from 1720 to 1726. Black operated a store and with his partner John Hyde in England, he acted as a factor for Maryland planters. When he returned to England in 1726, William Black became Dr. Carroll's principal London agent and the two men began 29 year exchange of business and personal letters.

[8] The Principio Iron Works was established on the North East River in Cecil County in 1719. Although the company had 12,000 acres in the area to supply iron ore and timber for charcoal, it purchased additional iron ore deposits on the Patapsco River in Baltimore County, and in 1728 brought Augustine Washington into the company in order to acquire his iron ore lands in Stafford County, Virginia. Augustine, Jr., George Washington's eldest brother, inherited the family's interest in the

Principio Company at his father's death in 1743.

The furnace was very successful and by the 1740's was supplying almost half of the pig iron exported to England from North America. During the American Revolution, the Principio Iron Works was confiscated as Tory property and sold to General Mordicai Gist and Robert Long of Baltimore.

Dr. Carroll's losses due to the two fires amounted to over £1,600. The January 14, 1746 issue of the *Maryland Gazette* reported: "On Saturday Evening last, a Fire broke out in a Warehouse belonging to Dr. *Charles Carroll,* in this City; which in about 2 Hours consumed the same, with a great many valuable Effects: There were several other Warehouses adjoining, which, by the Diligence of the Inhabitants, were with great Difficulty preserved. It is said the Damage amounts to upwards of 1000£ Sterling."

On September 9th of the same year the *Gazette* reported another fire, again completely destroying Dr. Carroll's warehouse with a loss of "upward of 600£ Sterling."

9 Dr. Carroll was buried next to his younger son in a vault in St. Anne's churchyard in Annapolis. In 1761 Charles Carroll, Barrister wrote to his agent in London for a marble slab to cover the vault. The Carroll arms were to be cut at the head of the stone, followed by an inscription. All trace of the stone has disappeared and it is believed that the monument to Margaret Tilghman Carroll, the Barrister's widow, now sits over the family vault.

CHAPTER II

1 In the eighteenth century the daily ration of rum in the British Navy was a half pint per seaman. If it is assumed that the rum ration to workmen on land was identical, the mathematical extension of the 38 gallons charged to the Barrister's account from June 26 to July 28, a period of 28 working days with Sundays excepted, indicates an average labor force of 21 or 22 workmen. It is interesting to note that in the early part of the eighteenth century British seamen normally received their full strength ration of rum at noon. After 1739, however, the half-pint ration was cut with a quart of water, and half of this beverage, known as "grog," was served twice daily, six hours apart. This latter practice was found necessary to assure that there be an able-bodied force to man the ship at all times.

2 In the Barrister's lifetime, the private room for master of the house was called a *study,* or "studdy." The use of the word *library* for such a room did not begin until the very late eighteenth century. Inventories and architectural plans of the first quarter of the nineteenth century rarely used the term library. An *office* was a place for transacting business—a room in which "clerkly work" was done. Charles Carroll's office at Mount Clare was

in the west flanking dependency and at Annapolis would have been in or near his warehouse on the harbor. In neither case would the Barrister's office have been in the house.

3 Handmade bricks used to form flat arches were often *rubbed* to give them smooth and even surfaces compared with the rougher texture of the bricks in the rest of the wall. Rubbing also gave the bricks a more uniform color. The bricks were also *gauged* or shaped to fit the radius of the arch. Rubbed and gauged bricks in flat arches were laid with narrower mortar joints than those used in the rest of the wall in order to increase the effect of their even color and texture.

4 Dr. Carroll's house at Conduit and Church Steets, and Reynolds' Tavern on Church Circle, built before 1742, are the two earliest surviving examples in Annapolis of buildings with all-header bond. The old rectory of St. Anne's Church and the Peggy Stewart house, both built in the early 1760's, the Ridout and Scott houses from the middle of the decade, and the James Brice house dating from the late 1760's were all constructed using all-header bond. In England this bond is known as Bastard Bond because of its wide use by the brothers, John and William Bastard, who were responsible for much of the rebuilding of Blandford in Dorset after the town burned in 1731.

5 The plantation originally consisted of two land patents, Sparrow's Rest, patented by Thomas Sparrow in 1652, and Sparrow's Addition, which he patented in 1673. When Nicholas Maccubbin purchased the property from Thomas' grandson, he added an adjacent patent, Squirrel Neck, and called his plantation by that name.

6 The capitals on the two story pilasters on Squirrel Neck are almost identical to those on the one story pilasters on Cedar Park, located three miles south of the Maccubbin house. Cedar Park was built as a frame, one-and-a-half story house in the latter part of the seventeenth century and brick walls, with a pilaster at each end of the river front, were added in the second quarter of the eighteenth century, probably about 1740. The pilasters on Cedar Park may be the earliest surviving examples in Maryland.

The capitals on the Squirrel Neck and Cedar Park pilasters are also nearly identical to those on Friendship Hall, near East New Market in Dorchester County. This brick house is believed to date from the 1740's or early 50's and originally to have been one-and-a-half stories, with a one story pilaster at each end of the entrance facade. After the Revolution, the house was raised to a full two stories.

Another notable construction feature of Squirrel Neck is the lack of both a belt course at the second floor level and a projecting water table below the first floor line. Both are usually found on eighteenth century masonry buildings. Also, the walls are laid in English bond of alternating courses of header and stretcher bricks instead of the usual Flemish bond.

Gambrel roofs were much more prevalent in all the American colonies in the seventeenth and eighteenth centuries than is often realized. A number of important mid-eighteenth century Maryland houses had gambrel roofs, Squirrel Neck being among the few surviving examples. Padsworth Farm at Queen Anne on the Patuxent River, seven miles from Squirrel Neck, was one of the major houses of its period, but has totally disappeared and today is known only through a series of sketches drawn by Francis Meyer sometime after the Civil War. Built by William Murdock, probably between 1735 and 1745, this two-and-a-half-story brick house had a gambrel roof and may well have influenced the design of Squirrel Neck. Padsworth Farm was a richly detailed house with fully paneled rooms. Its staircase was separated from the passage by a double arch which probably was the design source of the similar double arch at Tulip Hill nearby on the West River.

[7] At Mount Clare, the master-mason displayed his ability by his use of rubbed and gauged brickwork in the flat arches and glazed headers up the length of the pilasters to subtly enrich the visual delight of the major facade of the house.

[8] The entrance fronts of Mountaintown, built in the 1730's near Kells in County Meath, Ireland and of Kilbarchan in Renfrewshire, Scotland, dating from the middle of the eighteenth century, closely resemble the garden elevation of Mount Clare. Both of these houses have four giant pilasters with the center two supporting a pediment and, as on the Maryland examples, the capitals of their pilasters sit directly under their cornices, without either an architrave or frieze.

[9] Very few eighteenth century compositions of houses with their balancing dependencies have survived unaltered. Fires, new and more convenient kitchen wings built onto the houses, or the subdivision of the land around the houses have caused the changes. Although the arrangement of a pair of outbuildings at right angles to the house, and with the end walls of the dependencies aligned with the entrance front of the house was not uncommon in the eighteenth century, no examples survive in Maryland today. In Virginia, one survives in part at Kingsmill Plantation just outside of Williamsburg. The Governor's Palace in Williamsburg, rebuilt on its original foundations, also has this relationship of house and dependencies.

[10] The two parlors across the garden side of Charles Carroll of Annapolis's house in Annapolis retain portions of their plaster paneled walls, but these may date from the mid-1760's when he im-

ported a plasterer to install similar work in his plantation, Doughoregan Manor, or from the early 1770's when major alterations were made to the Annapolis house.

The two most important houses built in Annapolis in the early 1760's, the Ridout house and the Scott house, both have plaster paneled walls, as does the James Brice house dating from the end of that decade.

Unfortunately, the Daniel Dulany the Elder house in Annapolis and the Barrister's house have completely disappeared. Both were of a size and importance to have had similar paneling.

[11] In 1706 the upper portion of Talbot County, which included the Tilghmans' lands, became Queen Anne's County.

[12] Margaret Bennett Ward is an example of the close-knit relationships among the few families which economically, politically and socially controlled the Chesapeake region in the colonial period. She was the widow of Matthew Tilghman Ward who was a first cousin of Matthew Tilghman and she was a great-aunt of both Margaret Tilghman and Charles Carroll, Barrister.

The estate Mrs. Ward left would have provided Margaret Tilghman, by the time of her marriage, with an income equivalent to approximately $50,000 in 1980 dollars.

[13] The Prymont water and the Spaw water ordered were for relief from the illness, probably a form of malaria, from which the Barrister suffered all of his life. In the fall of 1762 he wrote: "I this summer made an Excursion as far as Boston in order to Escape my Troublesome annual visitant the fever and Ague but had not Been Returned to Annapolis four Days before I was seized with it in a more violent manner than at any of its former attacks and it still keeps Possession of me."

Anderson, in London, recommended "Tarr water" which the Barrister thereafter ordered from his agent, along with other mineral waters, always insisting that they be fresh or not sent.

CHAPTER III

[1] Through the courtesy of Miss Mary E. Williams, City Archivist of the City of Bristol, a search was made for surviving records of the firm of Sedgley Hilhouse and Randolph. It was hoped that the Barrister's original letter and sketch might still exist. Unfortunately neither the firm nor its papers are in existence. Miss Williams did find that the two senior partners were distinguished men of Bristol during the time Charles Carroll engaged in business transactions with the firm. Samuel Sedgely was a City Councillor and also served as Sheriff while William Hilhouse was a Warden of the Society of Merchant Venturers.

[2] A replica of the 1676 State House was built in St.

Mary's City at the time of Maryland's tricentennial in 1934. The building was recreated under the direction of the Baltimore architects Herbert G. Crisp, James R. Edmunds, Jr. and Horace W. Peaslee using the original construction contract. The 1705 State House in Annapolis looked like the earlier one in St. Mary's City with the exception that the roof terminated with a platform surrounded by a balustrade with a tall lantern in the center rather like that on the Governor's Palace in Williamsburg.

3 Although inventories show that there were large collections of books both at Mount Clare and at the house in Annapolis, surviving records do not list any architectural pattern books in Charles Carroll's library. All through the Barrister's correspondence with London agents, there are numerous orders for books and periodicals, but no architectural titles. It is known that a number of pattern books were in the libraries of the Brice and Lloyd families and in Charles Carroll of Annapolis's which would have been at the Barrister's disposal to borrow. Whoever designed the recently completed Ridout and Scott houses would have had a collection as well as the local masons and carpenters and joiners.

4 Newby Hall in Yorkshire was altered in the late 1750's in a similar manner to Mount Clare. To an existing late seventeenth century house, the architect, Carr of York, added a pair of one story advancing wings with polygonal ends, and designed an advancing center pavilion for the entrance facade between the new wings. Thus two architects working on opposite sides of the Atlantic solved the same problem of "modernizing" an earlier house into a Palladian villa in the same way.

5 Joseph Horatio Anderson was the original architect for the present State House in Annapolis. He also designed a residence for John Morton Jordon, overlooking the Severn River, which was razed long ago for expansion of the Naval Academy. Anderson's beautifully executed drawings for now demolished extensions to the wings at Governor Sharpe's Whitehall and for an octagonal horse barn at the same plantation still exist. Nothing is known of Joseph Horatio Anderson's origins or training except his reference in a letter to "my knowledge of several Courts of Europe." It is known that in March 1770 he was in Philadelphia and by April 1771 was working in Annapolis. During the winter of 1774-75 Anderson was living in Alexandria, Virginia. He died sometime before 1778, probably in Alexandria.

William Buckland arrived in Annapolis after Joseph Horatio Anderson. In the fall of 1771 Buckland moved up from Richmond County, Virginia to work on the interiors of Edward Lloyd IV's town house. The house had been begun two years earlier by Samuel Chase. By the time the walls and

roof were constructed, the project proved to be too ambitious for Chase's finances and he sold the unfinished house to Lloyd for £3,000. William Buckland's abilities were known to the Lloyds through his work on the interiors of Mount Airy, Mrs. Lloyd's father's house in Richmond County, Virginia.

6 "Love" was the captain whose ship, the *Betsy*, the Barrister often used and an older brother of the Reverend David Love. Governor Sharpe sailed on Captain Love's ship when he left Maryland in 1773 for England.

7 The Barrister was showing himself to be a proper English gentleman. The Downs are the waters in the Straits of Dover off the coast of Kent, between Deal and the Goodwin Sands. The "Gentlemen of the Downs," in eighteenth century parlance, were smugglers dealing in French goods whose services were used by all of the gentry within easy reach of the coast.

8 Mrs. Ambler was the former Mary Cary and the widow of Edward Ambler of Jamestown. Her sister, Sally, married George Fairfax and lived at Belvoir, next to Mount Vernon. Mrs. Ambler had traveled from Belvoir to Baltimore to have her children inoculated against smallpox by Dr. Henry Stevenson and was returning to Virginia when her coach broke down near the Baltimore Company's works. She and her children and servants stayed with the manager of the iron works and his wife, Mr. and Mrs. Clement Brooke, for several days until the coach was repaired and they could continue on their journey.

9 On April 11, 1775 Peale wrote from Baltimore to Charles Carroll, Barrister, in Annapolis: "I have been at work on your other Landscape & I hope to have it ready for the figures by next week, when I shall send them to Annapolis with Mrs. Peale." It is thought that the other landscape would have shown the entrance front of the house. Both landscapes hung in Mount Clare during the Barrister's and Mrs. Carroll's lifetimes, but there is no trace of the other painting today.

10 One of the greatest fears in the eighteenth century was of fires. Dr. Carroll suffered several heavy losses by fire and the November 10, 1774 issue of the *Maryland Gazette* reported a near loss to the Carroll family: "Last night, between seven and eight o'clock, a stable belonging to Mrs. Gaither, near the dock, full of hay and fodder, by some means took fire and was consumed to ashes: and although the wind bleu pretty fresh . . . and several other houses catched the flames . . . by the assistance of the engin, the vigilance of the inhabatants, and a number of gentlemen from the country, together with about twenty seamen . . . who on the first alarm were ordered on shore, all further damage was prevented. — The governor, with many gentlemen in town, exerted them-

selves greatly and did not leave the place until the danger was entirely over. Indeed there was the greatest reason to fear that the fire would not have been extinguished until it had reduced every building to the water, including the dwelling-house of Charles Carroll, Esq. Barrister."

The same issue of the *Gazette* reported that Governor Robert Eden had returned from England "On Tuesday last," where he had gone to help settle the estate of his late brother-in-law, the sixth Lord Baltimore.

[11] It was the height of fashion to be driven by postillions instead of a coachman and even Charles Carroll of Carrollton, heir to perhaps the largest fortune in the colonies, had to be content with a removable coachman's box when he ordered his post chariot in 1771.

[12] The history of the merchant firm of Wallace Davidson and Johnson has been chronicled by Edward C. Papenfuse in his book, *In Pursuit of Profit,* published by the Johns Hopkins University Press, 1975. In 1804, some years after the break-up of the partnership, Charles Wallace and John Muir, another partner, founded the Farmers' Bank of Maryland, the first bank in Annapolis. Joshua Johnson remained in London where his daughter, Louise Catherine, married John Quincy Adams in 1797.

[13] The Dulany family was among those who had to leave Annapolis because of their outspoken support of the Crown and of the proprietary government. At the outbreak of the Revolution Daniel Dulany the Younger moved with his family to his plantation, Hunting Ridge, three miles from Mount Clare on the Frederick Road.

Dulany was a year older than Charles Carroll, Barrister. His father had come to Maryland in 1703 from Queen's County, Ireland, and had become the outstanding lawyer in the province. His father was also one of the founding partners of the Baltimore Company. The younger Dulany attended Eton and Clare College, Cambridge and read law at the Middle Temple, the same education the Barrister was to have. His stepmother was Henrietta Maria Lloyd, a first cousin of the Barrister's mother and of both parents of Margaret Tilghman Carroll.

Unlike the Barrister, the Dulany family became bitter enemies of Charles Carroll of Annapolis and his son, Charles Carroll of Carrollton. The bitterness was so intense that Carrollton challenged one of the Dulanys to a duel which their intermediaries prevented only with great difficulty.

In 1781 much of the Dulany family's property was confiscated, including Hunting Ridge, and Daniel Dulany the Younger moved into Baltimore where he died in 1797.

[14] With all the information known about the Barrister and his wife, the lack of knowledge about their children seems especially strange. The earliest family reference to them is found in Judge Nicholas Brice's memoirs written in the 1840's. Judge Brice, a great-nephew of the Barrister, who knew both his great-uncle and aunt, stated only that "They had two children both of whom died in infancy." A younger sister of the judge, born in 1783, was named Margaret Clare after her cousin who had recently died.

[15] The General Assembly of 1783 of the Maryland legislature passed an act in accordance with the terms of the Barrister's will changing Nicholas and James Maccubbin's surname to Carroll and granting them use of the "Coat of Arms and Armorial Bearings of the Family of Carroll or O'Carroll." This was the first instance of an American legislature's granting the use of a coat-of-arms.

CHAPTER IV

[1] John Ridout's judgment of the Barrister is exemplified by Carroll's moderation and calming influence in October 1774, during the mob action in Annapolis which resulted in the burning of the brigantine *Peggy Stewart* on the nineteenth. Anthony Stewart, who was evidently an obdurate Scot as well as a Loyalist, permitted tea to be sent aboard one of his ships after the non-importation agreement was in effect, and paid duty on the tea when it arrived in Annapolis on the fifteenth of that month. A rival merchant in London had sent word ahead to his partners in Annapolis to inform them of the tea aboard the *Peggy Stewart.* Stewart, along with James and Joseph Williams, to whom the tea was consigned, was ordered to appear before the Committee of Correspondence. The more fiery of the Revolutionists sent handbills through Anne Arundel and Baltimore Counties about the meeting and what a contemporary writer described as a "riotous mob . . . headed by a few hott headed Men" assembled. Mathias Hammond and Charles Carroll, Barrister, both of whom were on the Committee, proposed that the tea be publicly burned, but the mob leaders, who happened also to be rival merchants of the Williamses and Stewart, threatened to bring 3,000 more men into Annapolis in order to hang Stewart, pull down his house and burn his ship. "This they were diverted from," wrote Thomas Ringgold, who was not sympathetic toward Anthony Stewart, "by the Influence of Barrister Carroll and others in pity to Mrs. Stewart who was then in Labour." Stewart was forced finally to set fire to his own ship. John Galloway reporting the events to his father estimated the loss to Stewart at "900 pounds Current Money."

[2] Matthew Tilghman was one of the most distinguished and influential legislators in Maryland both before and during the Revolution. Tilghman had been elected one of Maryland's delegates to the Continental Convention of 1776-77 but did not

attend the convention in Philadelphia, believing that his duties as Chairman of the Maryland convention were a greater obligation. Thus he missed the opportunity to pen his signature, along with Maryland's other four delegates, to the Declaration of Independence.

[3] Annapolis had been laid out in 1683-84 into 100 one-acre lots. At the time of his death, the Barrister owned seven lots, making him the fourth largest property holder in the city. Together, these four property owners held 60 of the 100 lots, with Charles Carroll of Carrollton owning 28, Benedict Calvert holding 15, and Daniel Dulany, Sr. with 10.

CHAPTER V

[1] Baltimore had overtaken Annapolis in size well before the Revolution. In 1776 its population was over 6,700—more than double that of Annapolis. The first Federal census in 1790 put the population of Baltimore at 13,500; by 1810 the city had grown to 46,500.

[2] The earliest known orangery in Maryland was built circa 1755, at Wye House in Talbot County, and enlarged to its present size in 1779. This is the only orangery in Maryland to have survived intact.

In the eighteenth century there were also orangeries at Government House and at Dr. Scott's in Annapolis, and at Belair, the Ogle plantation in Prince George's County.

John Ridgely built an orangery at Hampton in Baltimore County shortly after he inherited the estate from his father in 1829. This was the last orangery built in Maryland. It burned in the mid-1920's and was reconstructed on its original foundations in 1976.

Just as the heating system of the Carrolls' orangery was an improvement over the earlier one used at Wye House, so the heating system at the Hampton orangery was an attempted improvement over the type at Mount Clare. At Hampton the floor was wood instead of brick, stone or dirt as in the earlier examples. The air space under the wood floor permitted air heated by the perimeter masonry hot air duct to radiate under the entire floor.

[3] Mount Clare was never a plantation house in the typical sense with the owner's residence surrounded by a village of outbuildings. This type of site plan, as seen for example at Mount Vernon, with its service lanes of buildings, including a spinning and weaving house and cobbler's shop and quarters for the plantation workers, did not exist at Mount Clare. The 1798 Federal Direct Tax, which listed each house and its outbuildings within a two-acre area around the house for each property in the country, has only the mansion with its connected dependencies and two outbuild-

ings for Mount Clare. The two one story stone outbuildings, each 20 by 20 feet, were the smoke house and the dairy house. An early twentieth century photograph shows the old pump, located on the site of the kitchen yard, within its octagonal wood housing. The handsome wood housing was about 18 inches in diameter and almost seven feet tall, topped by a wood acorn. Thomas H. Poppleton's map of Baltimore, published in 1823, indicates what were probably the stables and coach house to the northeast of the house. The farm buildings were well away from the main house, perhaps clustered near the overseer's house, the location of which is unknown.

[4] Starting in the summer of 1977, a series of archaeological digs have been conducted at Mount Clare. The work has revealed that extensive remains of the two flanking dependencies as well as the numerous outbuildings exist under the lawn around the house. A large number of artifacts have been recovered which, along with the invoices of the Barrister's and the surviving furnishings, will greatly aid in interpreting the life of the Carrolls at Mount Clare. A report of the archaeological work to date is being prepared by Norma Baumgartner-Wagner, the archaeologist directing the digs.

[5] Mrs. Carroll would have become familiar with this arrangement of rooms while in England. Also, several Annapolis houses which were either built or altered on the eve of the Revolution had this arrangement: Governor Eden's residence, the Chase-Lloyd house and the Ogles' house. A number of the new Federal villas built on the outskirts of Baltimore in the 1780's and 90's had three major rooms for entertaining.

[6] As Baltimore grew closer, these suburban villas were swallowed up by the tide of rowhouses. Willow Brook alone survived, as the House of the Good Shepherd, until 1965. Then, with demolition imminent, the Baltimore Museum of Art rescued the oval parlor, with its superb neoclassical plasterwork. The room is now in the museum's American Wing.

In 1804 Francis Guy painted a view of the city from Beech Hill. Baltimore and its harbor are to the southeast while to the southwest can be seen the roof of Willow Brook and the wooded land of Mount Clare reaching down to the river. This painting is also on exhibit in the American Wing of the Baltimore Museum of Art.

CHAPTER VI

[1] As with the Carroll family, an important part of Captain Ridgely's fortune came from his interest in an iron works, the Northhampton Furnace, ten miles above Baltimore. The Captain, also, built a country house, which he named Hampton, on part of the iron works tract. Built between 1783

and 1790, Hampton was the largest house in Maryland at the time of its completion.

[2] Mount Clare Station, at Pratt and Poppleton Streets, and the roundhouse adjoining it, which was built in 1883, form the Baltimore and Ohio Transportation Museum.

[3] John Contee renamed the plantation Java in honor of the naval battle in which he participated. In December 1812 the *USS Constitution*, on which John Contee was serving, defeated and sank the *HMS Java* off the coast of Brazil. A tradition in the Contee family says that he paid for the land with prize money earned while he served aboard the *USS Constitution* during the War of 1812.

[4] Harry Dorsey Gough Carroll did not inherit any of his father's estate since, by prior arrangement within the family, he inherited the bulk of the property of his grandfather, Harry Dorsey Gough. This legacy included Perry Hall with its 1,300 acres.

[5] Achsah Ridgely Carroll also inherited $13,000 in cash, 1,074 acres in Baltimore County, several houses on Gay Street near Market Street (now Baltimore Street), and her father's town house on Gay Street.

[6] The house numbers were changed later in the nineteenth century. In the 1850's Enoch Pratt's house, now part of the Maryland Historical Society, at the southeast corner of the same block, was number 87 West Monument Street. Today it is 201 West Monument Street.

[7] The citizens of Baltimore owe a debt of gratitude to the acquisition policy of the Park Board. As a number of the remaining early nineteenth century country seats came on the market, they were acquired for public open spaces. In addition to Mount Clare, the purchase of Druid Hill in 1860, Clifton in 1895, and Montebello in the early twentieth century are examples of this policy.

[8] During this work in 1908, the original entrance to the basement was found, as well as parts of the masonry walls and brick paving of the extension to it added by Mrs. Margaret Carroll in the 1780's. When the east hyphen and wing had been demolished 37 years earlier, these had been filled in and forgotten. Their discovery gave rise to romantic stories of a secret passage, flights from Indian attacks, and smuggled goods. When the road next to the east wing was built at the same time, workmen came upon the sunken portion of the eighteenth century icehouse which added another dimension to the tales of the secret passage with a tunnel leading to a secret room.

Adams, John. *The Diary and Autobiography of John Adams.* 4 vols. Edited by H. L. Butterfield, Cambridge, Mass.: Belknap Press of Harvard University, 1961

Akerman, James B. "Eleutherian Mills Garden Site." *Historical Archaeology,* 2 (1968), pp. 69-72

Ambler, Mary. "Diary of M. Ambler, 1770." *Virginia Magazine of History and Biography.* XLV (1937), pp. 152-170

The Baltimore Museum of Art. *"Anywhere So Long As there be Freedom," Charles Carroll of Carrollton, His Family & His Maryland.* Baltimore: The Baltimore Museum of Art. 1975 (Catalogue of an exhibition at the Baltimore Museum of Art)

Baltz, Shirley V. *The Quays of the City, An Account of the bustling Eighteenth Century Port of Annapolis.* Annapolis: The Liberty Tree, Ltd., 1975

————. *Belle Air in Bowie, Its Families & History.* Bowie, Md. Bowie American Revolution Bicentennial Committee, 1977

Beirne, Rosamond Randall. "Two Anomalous Annapolis Architects: Joseph Horatio Anderson and Robert Key." *Maryland Historical Magazine,* 55 (1960), pp. 183-200

————. and Scarff, John Henry, F.A.I.A. *William Buckland, 1734-1774, Architect of Virginia and Maryland.* Baltimore: The Maryland Historical Society, 1958

Berkley, Henry J. "Colonial Ruins, Colonial Architecture and Brickwork of the Chesapeake Bay Section." *Maryland Historical Magazine* XIX (1924), pp. 1-10

Bevan, Edith Rossiter. "Gardens and Gardening in Early Maryland." *Maryland Historical Magazine,* XLV (1950), pp. 243-270

Craig, Maurice. *Classic Irish Houses of the Middle Size.* London: The Architectural Press Ltd., 1976

Cruickshank, Dan and Wyld, Peter. *London: The Art of Georgian Building.* London: The Architectural Press Ltd., 1975

Coffin, Lewis A. Jr. and Holden, Arthur C. *Brick Architecture of the Colonial Period in Maryland and Virginia.* New York: Architectural Book Publishing Co., 1919

Davis, Deering. *Annapolis Houses, 1700-1775.* New York: Architectural Book Publishing Co., Inc., 1947

Day, Alan F. "A Social Study of Lawyers in Maryland, 1660-1775." Ph.D. dissertation, The Johns Hopkins University, 1976

Delaplaine, Edward S. "The Life of Thomas Johnson." Parts Seventh, Eighth and Tenth. *Maryland Historical Magazine,* XV (1920), pp. 324-341; XVI (1921), pp. 260-279; XVII (1922), pp. 191-209

Dutton, Ralph. *The Age of Wren.* London: B. T. Batsford Ltd., 1951

Elder, William Voss III. *Maryland Queen Anne and Chippendale Furniture of the Eighteenth Century.* Baltimore: The Baltimore Museum of Art, 1968 (Catalogue of an exhibition at the Baltimore Museum of Art)

————. *Baltimore Painted Furniture 1800-1840.* Baltimore: The Baltimore Museum of Art, 1972 (Catalogue of an exhibition at the Baltimore Museum of Art)

Elwell, Newton W. *Architecture, Furniture and Interiors of Maryland and Virginia During the Eighteenth Century.* Boston: Geroge H. Polley, 1897

"Extracts from the Carroll Papers." *Maryland Historical Magazine,* XII (1917), pp. 276-296, 347-369

Fisher, Richard D. "The Burning of the 'Peggy Stewart.'" *Maryland Historical Magazine* 5 (1910): pp. 235-245

Fisher, William H. *Some Old Houses of Maryland.* Oxford, Md.: By Mrs. William H. Fisher, 1979

Forman, Henry Chandlee. *Early Manor and Plantation Houses of Maryland.* Easton, Md.: By the author, 1934

————. *Old Buildings, Gardens, and Furniture in Tidewater Maryland.* Cambridge, Md.: Tidewater Publishers, 1967

Francis, Raymond. *Looking for Georgian England.* London: Macdonald & Co., 1952

Gary, Joy. "Patrick Creagh of Annapolis." *Maryland Historical Magazine,* XLVIII (1953), pp. 310-326

Girouard, Mark. *Life in the English Country House, A Social and Architectural History.* New Haven: Yale University Press, 1978

Griffith, Thomas W. *Annals of Baltimore.* Baltimore: William Wooddy, 1833

Harley, R. Bruce. "Dr. Charles Carroll — Land Speculator, 1730-1755." *Maryland Historical Magazine,* 46 (1951), pp. 93-107

Hollifield, William. *Difficulties Made Easy, History of the Turnpikes of Baltimore City and County.* Cockeysville, Md.: Baltimore County Historical Society, 1978

Holt, W. Stull, "Charles Carroll, Barrister: The Man." *Maryland Historical Magazine*, XXXI (1936), pp. 112-126

Hughes, Rupert. *George Washington.* 3 vols. New York: William Morrow & Company, 1926, 1927, 1930

Hume, Ivor Noel. *Historical Archaeology.* New York: Alfred A. Knopf, 1969

Hunter, Wilber Harvey, Jr. *Mount Clare, HABS No. MD-192.* Historic American Buildings Survey, 1960

Irvin, Robert, ed. *Baltimore, 200th Anniversary, 1729-1929.* Baltimore: Baltimore Municipal Journal, 1929

Ison, Walter. *The Georgian Buildings of Bath, 1700 to 1830.* London: Farber and Farber, Ltd., 1948

Johnson, Keach. "Genesis of the Baltimore Ironworks." *Journal of Southern History,* 19 (no. 2, May 1953), pp. 157-179

Kimball, Fiske. *Domestic Architecture of the American Colonies and of the Early Republic.* New York: Charles Scribner's Sons, 1922

Lees-Milne, James. *The Age of Adam.* London: B. T. Batsford Ltd., 1947

"Letters of Charles Carroll, Barrister." *Maryland Historical Magazine* 31 (1936) through 38 (1943), *passim.*

Lord, Walter. *The Dawn's Early Light.* New York: W. W. Norton & Company, Inc., 1972

McCauley, Lois B. *Maryland Historical Prints, 1752-1889.* Baltimore: The Maryland Historical Society, 1975

McGrain, John W. *Grist Mills in Baltimore County, Maryland.* Towson, Md.: Baltimore County Public Library, 1980

McWilliams, Jane and Papenfuse, Edward. *Appendix F, Lot Histories and Maps, Vol II, NEH Grant #H 69-0-178.* Annapolis, 1971, on deposit at the Maryland Hall of Records

Marye, William B. "The Old Indian Road." *Maryland Historical Magazine*, XV (1920), pp. 107-124

——. "Some Baltimore City Place Names." *Maryland Historical Magazine,* 54 (1959), pp. 15-35

Maryland, A Guide to the Old Line State. New York: Oxford University Press, 1940

Maryland Historical Society. Mark Alexander Accounts, MS 11

——. Dr. Charles Carroll Letterbooks, MS 208

——. James Carroll and James Carroll, Jr. Accounts, MS 217

——. Carroll-Maccubbin Papers, MS 219

——. Tench Tilghman Accounts, MS 1445

Miller, Phillip. *The Gardners Dictionary.* 7th edition. London: 1749

Mount Vernon, An Illustrated Handbook. Mount Vernon, Va.: The Mount Vernon Ladies Association of the Union, 1972

An Old Gardener. *The Practical American Gardener.* Baltimore: Fielding Lucus, Jr., 1819

Paul, J. G. D. "A Lost Copy-book of Charles Carroll of Carrollton." *Maryland Historical Magazine,* XXXII (1937), pp. 193-225

Papenfuse, Edward C. *In Pursuit of Profit, The Annapolis Merchants in the Era of the American Revolution, 1763-1805.* Baltimore: The Johns Hopkins University Press, 1975

——. Day, Alan F.; Jordan, David W.; and Stiverson, Gregory A. *A Biographical Dictionary of the Maryland Legislature, 1635-1789.* Vol. 1: A-H. Baltimore: The Johns Hopkins University Press, 1979

——. Stiverson, Gregory A.; Collins, Susan A.; and Carr, Lois Green, ed. *Maryland, A New Guide to the Old Line State.* Baltimore: The Johns Hopkins University Press, 1976

Park, Helen. "A List of Architectural Books Available in America before the Revolution." *Journal of the Society of Architectural Historians,* XX (October 1961), pp. 115-130

Pevsner, Nikolaus. *An Outline of European Architecture.* 7th ed. London: Penguin Books Ltd., 1963

Radoff, Morris L. *Buildings of the State of Maryland at Annapolis.* Annapolis: The Hall of Records Commission, State of Maryland, 1954

——. *The State House at Annapolis.* Annapolis: The Hall of Records Commission, State of Maryland, 1972

Raley, Robert L. "Early American Plasterwork and Stuccowork." *Journal of the Society of Architectural Historians,* XX (October 1961), pp. 131-135

Ridgely, David. *Annals of Annapolis.* Baltimore: Cushing & Brother, 1841

Ridout, Orlando IV. *The James Brice House, Annapolis,* M.A. thesis, University of Maryland, 1978

Ridout Papers, D371. Gift Collection, Hall of Records, Annapolis

Roth, Rodris. *The Interior Decoration of City Houses in Baltimore, 1783-1812.* M.A. thesis, University of Delaware, 1956

Scarlett, Charles, Jr. "Governor Horatio Sharpe's Whitehall." *Maryland Historical Magazine,* XLVI (1951), pp. 8-26

Scharf, J. Thomas. *The Chronicles of Baltimore.* Baltimore: Turnbull Brothers, 1874

——. *History of Baltimore City and County.* Philadelphia: Louis H. Everts, 1881

Seale, William. *Recreating the Historic House Interior.* Nashville: American Association for State and Local History, 1979

Sellers, Charles Coleman. *Charles Willson Peale with Patron and Populace, A Supplement to Portraits and Miniatures by Charles Willson*

Peale, With a Survey of his Work in Other Genres. Philadelphia: The American Philosophical Society, 1969

Shomette, Donald. Londontown, A Brief History. Londontown, Md.: London Town Publik House Commission, Inc., 1978

Sioussat, Mrs. Albert. Mount Clare, Carroll Park, Baltimore. Baltimore: Maryland Society of the Colonial Dames of America, 1926

Sioussant, Annie Leaken. "An Old Carroll Homestead." Antiquarian, 2 (no. 6, July 1924), pp. 24-25

South, Stanley. The Paca House, Annapolis, Maryland, A Historical Archaeological Study. Annapolis: 1967

Stiverson, Gregory A., and Jacobsen, Phebe R. William Paca, A Biography. Baltimore: The Maryland Historical Society, 1976

Summerson, John. Georgian London. New York: Charles Scribner's Sons, 1946

————. Architecture in Britain, 1530-1830. London: Penguin Books, Ltd., 5th ed. 1969; reprint ed., Baltimore: Penguin Books, Inc., 1970

Swanson, Neil H. The Perilous Fight. New York: Farrar and Rinehart, 1945

Tatum, George B. Philadelphia Georgian, The City House of Samuel Powel and Some of Its Eighteenth-Century Neighbors. Middletown, Conn.: Wesleyan University Press, 1976

Thirty-Second Annual Report of the Public Park Commission to the Mayor and City Council of Baltimore, for the Fiscal Year Ending December 31, 1891. Baltimore: A Hoen & Co., 1892

Thomas, Dawn F. and Barnes, Robert. The Green Spring Valley, Its History and Heritage. 2 Vols. Baltimore: The Maryland Historical Society, 1978

Tilghman, Harrison, ed. "Letters Between the English and American Branches of the Tilghman Family, 1697-1764." Maryland Historical Magazine, XXXIII (1938), pp. 148-175

Tilghman, J. Donnell. "Bill for the Construction of the Chase House." Maryland Historical Magazine, XXXIII (1938), pp. 23-26

Wainwright, Nicholas B. Colonial Grandeur in Philadelphia, The House and Furniture of General John Cadwalader. Philadelphia: The Histor-

ical Society of Pennsylvania, 1964

Wallace, Davidson and Johnson Letterbooks, 1507 and 1508. Hall of Records, Annapolis

Warren, Marion E. and Warren, Mary Elizabeth. The Train's Done Been Gone," An Annapolis Portrait, 1859-1910. Boston: David R. Godine, 1976

Warren, Mary G. and Warren, Marion E. Annapolis Adventure. Annapolis: By the authors, 1970

Washington, George. The Diaries of George Washington. 4 vols. Edited by John C. Fitzpatrick. New York: Houghton Mifflin Company, 1925

————. The Writings of George Washington from the Original Manuscript Sources, 1745-1799. 39 vols. Edited by John C. Fitzpatrick. Washington: United States Government Printing Office, 1931-1944.

Waterman, Thomas Tileston. The Mansions of Virginia, 1706-1776. Chapel Hill: The University of North Carolina Press, 1946

————. The Dwellings of Colonial America. Chapel Hill: The University of North Carolina Press, 1950

Wheeler, Joseph Towne. "Booksellers and Circulation Libraries in Colonial Maryland." Maryland Historical Magazine, XXXIV (1939), pp. 111-137

————. "Books Owned by Marylanders, 1700-1776." Maryland Historical Magazine, XXXV (1940), pp. 337-353

————. "Reading Interests of the Professional Classes in Colonial Maryland, 1700-1776." Maryland Historical Magazine, XXXVI (1941), pp. 181-201, 281-301

————. "Reading Interests of Maryland Planters and Merchants, 1700-1776." Maryland Historical Magazine, XXXVII (1942), pp. 26-41, 291-310

Whiffen, Marcus. The Eighteenth-Century Houses of Williamsburg. Williamsburg: Colonial Williamsburg, 1960

Wilstach, Paul. Tidewater, Maryland. Indianapolis: The Bobbs-Merrill Company, 1931

Yarwood, Doreen. The Architecture of England. London: B. T. Batsford Ltd., 1963

GLOSSARY OF ARCHITECTURAL TERMS

All header bond: A method of laying brick in which all courses are laid as headers.

Architrave: The lowest member of an entablature which rests upon the capital of a column. Also, the molded band, group of moldings, or other finished work surrounding a door or window. See also Casing and Surround.

Barge board: The board following the rake or slope of a gable underneath the overhanging shingle or slate.

Belt course: A projecting course or courses on the exterior of a building, usually at a floor level.

Bristol glass: See Crown glass.

Bulkhead: A horizontal or sloping structure providing access to a basement stairway.

Bulls-eye window: A circular window.

Capital: The uppermost part or head of a column, pilaster, or pier.

Casing: The framework around a window or door. See also Architrave and Surround.

Chair rail: A molding on a wall at the height of a chair back to protect the wall from damage.

Chamfer: To cut away the edge of a corner at a 45 degree angle.

Composition ornament: Ornament made of gesso, a composition of plaster of Paris and glue, and applied to a surface. The pieces of ornament are usually cast in molds.

Cornice: The uppermost part of an entablature usually used to crown the wall of a building.

Course: In masonry construction, a continuous horizontal range of brick or stone.

Crosette: A projection or ear at a corner of the architrave. Also known as a "knee."

Crown glass: The most widely used glass for glazing in the eighteenth century. Crown glass was formed by the glassblower spinning a glass bubble

in one hand and with the other beating the bubble into a disk about four feet in diameter. The circular sheet, or table, of glass would then be cut into panes. Bristol glass was a greatly inferior type of glass, not as clear and with imperfections. Bristol glass sold for less than half the price of the best crown glass.

Dependencies: The minor or flanking buildings of an architectural composition.

Diocletian window: A window within an arched opening, divided into three sections by two vertical posts. The name is derived from the use of this type of window in the Baths of Diocletian, constructed between 298 and 305 in Rome. Diocletian windows were later used by such influential architects as Andrea Palladio and James Gibbs.

Eaves: The lower edges of the roof which extend beyond the walls.

Engaged column: A column which is built one-third or one-quarter into a wall, the remainder projecting beyond and free from the face or the wall.

English Baroque: The style of Renaissance architecture introduced into England by Inigo Jones (1573-1652) before the Civil War. The style flourished after the Restoration under the leadership of Sir Christopher Wren (1632-1723) and culminated with the work of Sir John Vanbrugh (1664-1726).

English bond: A method of laying brick in which one course is laid with stretchers and the next with headers, thus bonding the thickness of brick together.

Entablature: The upper section of a classical order, resting on the capital and consisting of the cornice, frieze and architrave.

Facade: The face or elevation of a building.

Falls: The term used in Maryland and Virginia for earth terraces in a garden. A series of such terraces forms a "falling garden."

Federal period: The period in American architecture dating from the close of the American Revolution in 1783 until shortly after the War of 1812.

Fielded panel: A panel with a wide, flat surface.

Finial: A terminating ornament used on the apex of gables, pediments, roofs, etc.

Flat arch: An arch whose underside is flat.

Flemish bond: A method of laying brick in which headers and stretchers alternate in each course. Vertically, headers are placed over stretchers to form a bond.

Fluting: The surface of a pilaster or column which is enriched with vertical channeling.

Folly: An ornamental building or structure, often of a decorative or fanciful shape.

Forecourt: The area before a building which is enclosed by flanking buildings or walls.

Freize: The portion of the entablature between the architrave and the cornice.

Frontispiece: An architectural treatment of an entrance motive.

Gambrel: A roof having its shape broken by an obtuse angle so that the lower slope is steeper than the upper.

Gauged brick: Bricks which have been cut with a bricklayer's saw, then rubbed to a desired shape. When used in an arch, the joints of gauged bricks radiate from a common center.

Georgian period: The period in American architecture dating from the beginning of the reign of George I in 1714 until the beginning of the American Revolution in 1775. The mid-Georgian period is considered to have been between 1750 and 1765.

Giant pilaster: A pilaster two stories or more in height.

Head: Top of a window, door, or arch.

Header: The end of a brick; a brick laid across the thickness of a wall with an end towards the face of the wall.

Hyphen: A structure, often serving as a passage, connecting a dependency to a house.

Jamb: The side or lining of a doorway or window.

Joiner: One who does finish or ornamental carpentry.

Keystone: The wedge-shaped piece at the crown of an arch, so called because it is set last and binds or locks together all the other members of the arch.

Lantern: A cupola or small structure, sometimes of considerable height, on a roof, with openings or windows.

Lights: Window panes.

Lintel: The horizontal top piece of a window or door opening.

Loggia: A roofed but open gallery or arcade on a building.

Lunette window: An arched or rounded window.

Modillion: An ornamental block, applied to the underside of the projecting members of a cornice.

Molded: Enriched with decorative shapes or designs.

Mullion: A narrow wood or stone division between window openings.

Muntin: The horizontal and vertical members in window sashes used to divide the glass.

Newel or Newel post: The post placed at the first or lowest step to support the handrail.

Ogee: A molding with an S-shaped curve formed by the union of concave and convex lines.

Outbuilding: A building separate from, but associated with, a main building.

Pale: A stake, stick, or picket.

Paling: A fence made of pales or pickets.

Palisade: An enclosure of stakes or pickets (i.e., pales), sometimes mounted on a low masonry wall.

Palladian: A style of Renaissance architecture founded upon the work of the Italian architect Andrea Palladio (1508-1580), who worked in Vicenza and Venice. Anglo-Palladian is the architectural style derived from that of Palladio which flowered in Britain and her colonies in the eighteenth century.

Palladian window: See Venetian window.

Pattern-book: The term used for manuals and books published from the seventeenth to the nineteenth centuries dealing with the theory and practice of architecture and building.

Paver: A stone or brick used in a road, pavement, or floor. Brick pavers are sometimes square in shape and often thinner than regular building bricks.

Pavilion: A projecting motive on a facade to give architectural emphasis.

Pedestal: An architectural support or base.

Pediment: A crowning motive of porticos, pavilions, doorways, or other architectural features, usually of low triangular form resembling a gable.

Piazza: A veranda or porch.

Pilaster: A flat form of a column applied to a wall and projecting from the wall about a fourth or a sixth of its width.

Portico: An open space or colonade with a roof supported by columns, usually attached to a building as a porch, but sometimes detached.

Roman Doric: The Roman Doric order differs from the Greek in having a proportionately longer column shaft, by the addition of an astragal around the shaft slightly below the capital and in having a base.

Rubbed brick: Brick usually selected for an even color and rubbed to a smooth surface on the exposed faces.

Rustication: An emphasis of the joints of stonework done by deeply recessing them in a square or chamfered groove. The same treatment is imitated in woodwork and stuccowork.

Segmental arch: An arch whose curve is less than a semicircle.

Semioctagonal: Half octagonal in shape.

Shaft: That part of column between the capital and the base.

Stretcher: The long face of a brick.

Surround: The ornamental work around an opening, see Architrave and Casing.

Venetian window: A group of three windows, the central one of which is wider and taller than the others and is roundheaded. The two side windows are squareheaded.

Villa: The term used in the eighteenth century to denote a country seat or suburban residence of architectural distinction and elegance.

Water table: A projection of the lower masonry or brickwork on the exterior or a wall, at or near the first floor level.